snapped

© Éditions Assouline
26 rue Danielle-Casanova 75002 Paris
Tel: 33 1 42 60 33 84 Fax: 33 1 42 60 33 85

Printed and bound in Switzerland

First edition

snapped

PHOTOS OF THE AGENCE FRANCE-PRESSE

(Cover)
NEW YORK, United States, 10 June 1991
Parade on Broadway after "Operation Desert Storm"
It's a dog's life . . .

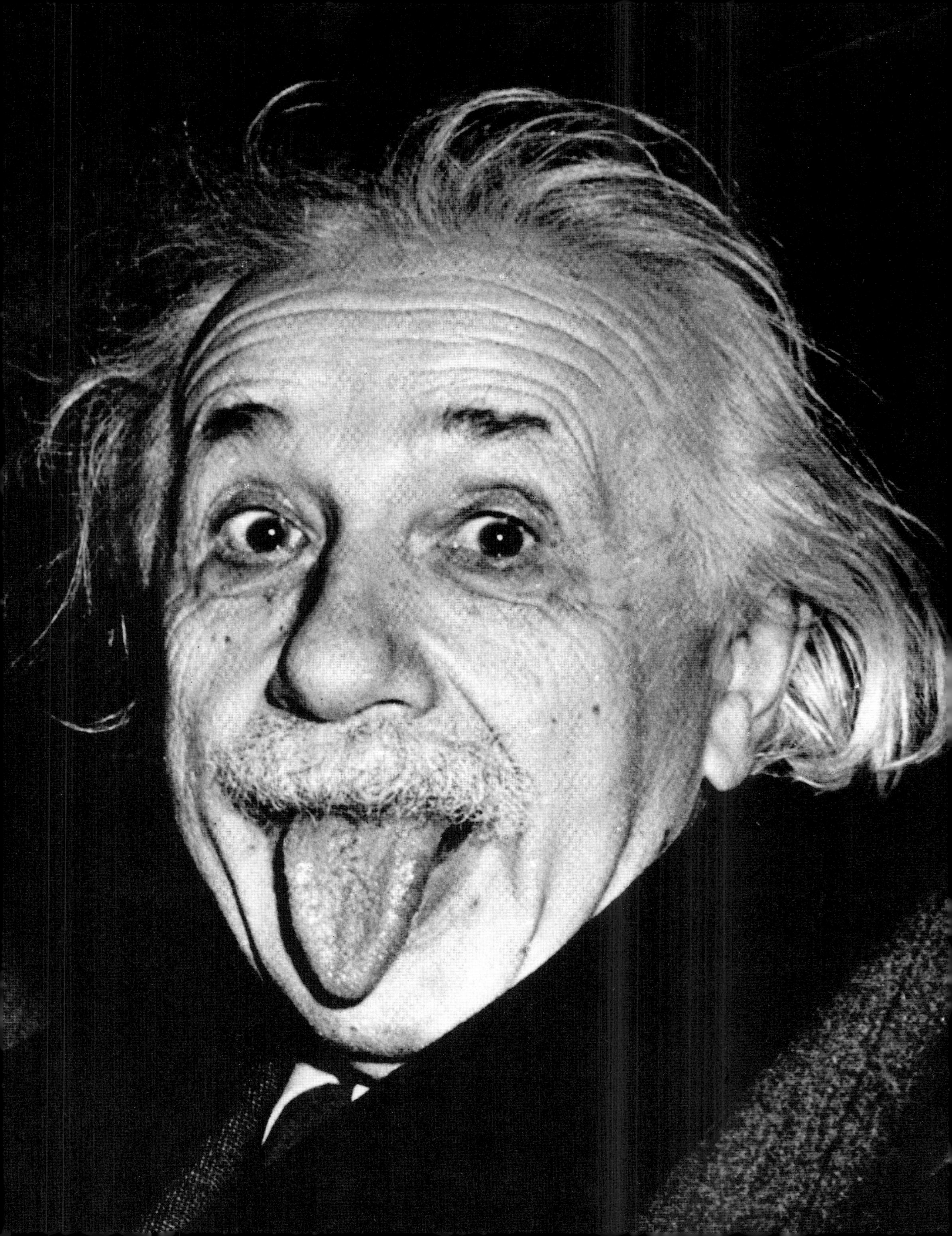

Products of the powerful worldwide media machine, Agence France-Presse, these photographs are moments of laughter stolen from current affairs. Hidden in the AFP's formidable arhives − 70,000 photographs taken every year by 150 photojournalists, and a total of seven million pictures on file, ready to be sent via one of six satellites to newspaper offices throughout the world, − lies a veritable treasure trove of amusing images. Some of them have already been around the world several times, becoming famous stars, like Einstein sticking his tongue out, or Clinton's cat, Socks, assailed by the paparazzi. Most of them, however, are totally unknown, because the press tends to prefer more serious pictures . . . No mattter, while news goes out of date, the timeless quality of humour guarantees these shots' immortality.

18 March 1951
The expression of genius. This irreverent picture of Albert Einstein, taken on his 72nd birthday, became world famous.

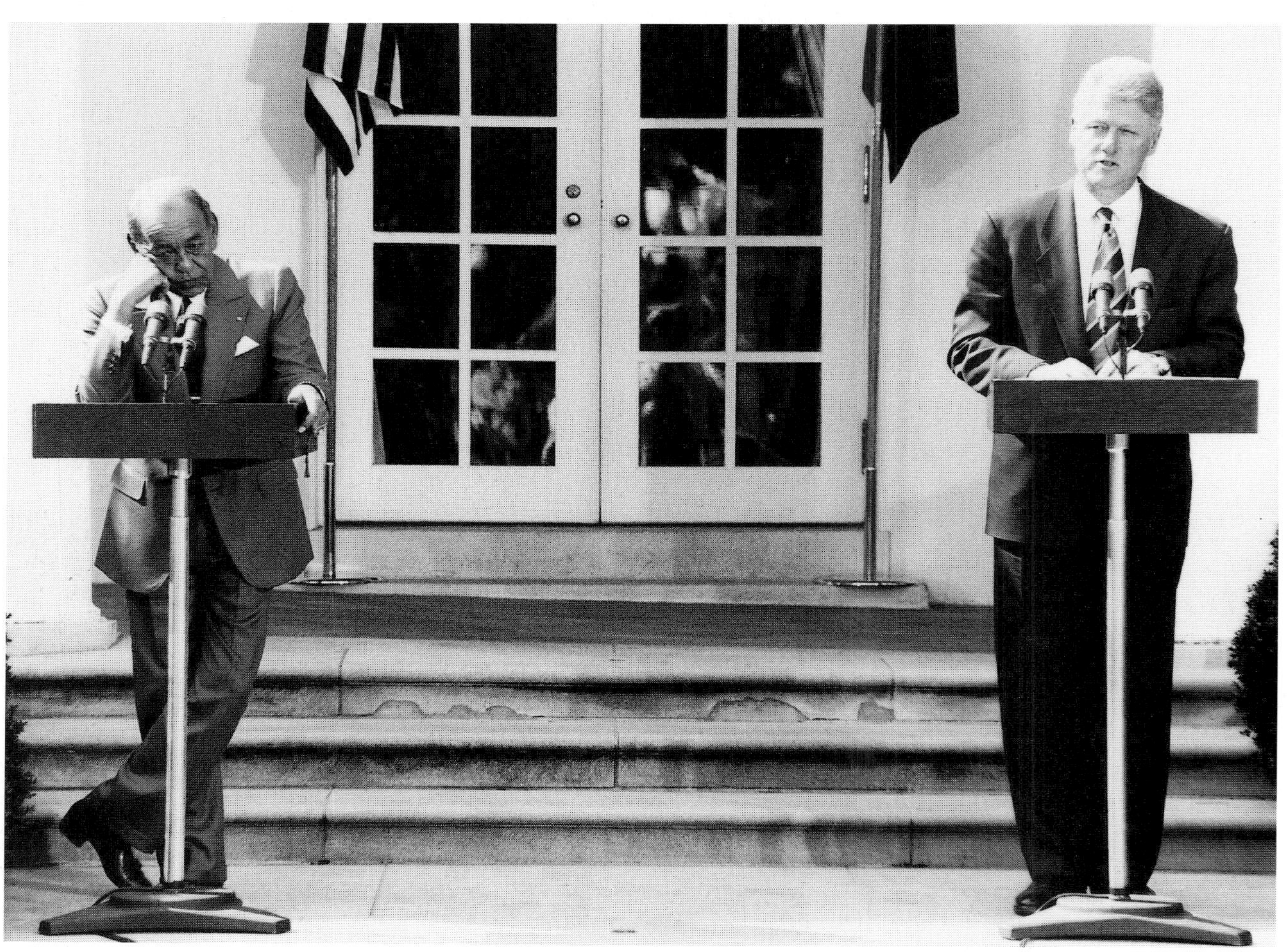

WASHINGTON, United States, 15 March 1995
Bill Clinton receives Hassan II
Not that old tune again . . .

MARRAKESH, Morocco, 28 January 1983
François Mitterrand is the guest of Hassan II
. . . makes quite an effective lullaby, though.

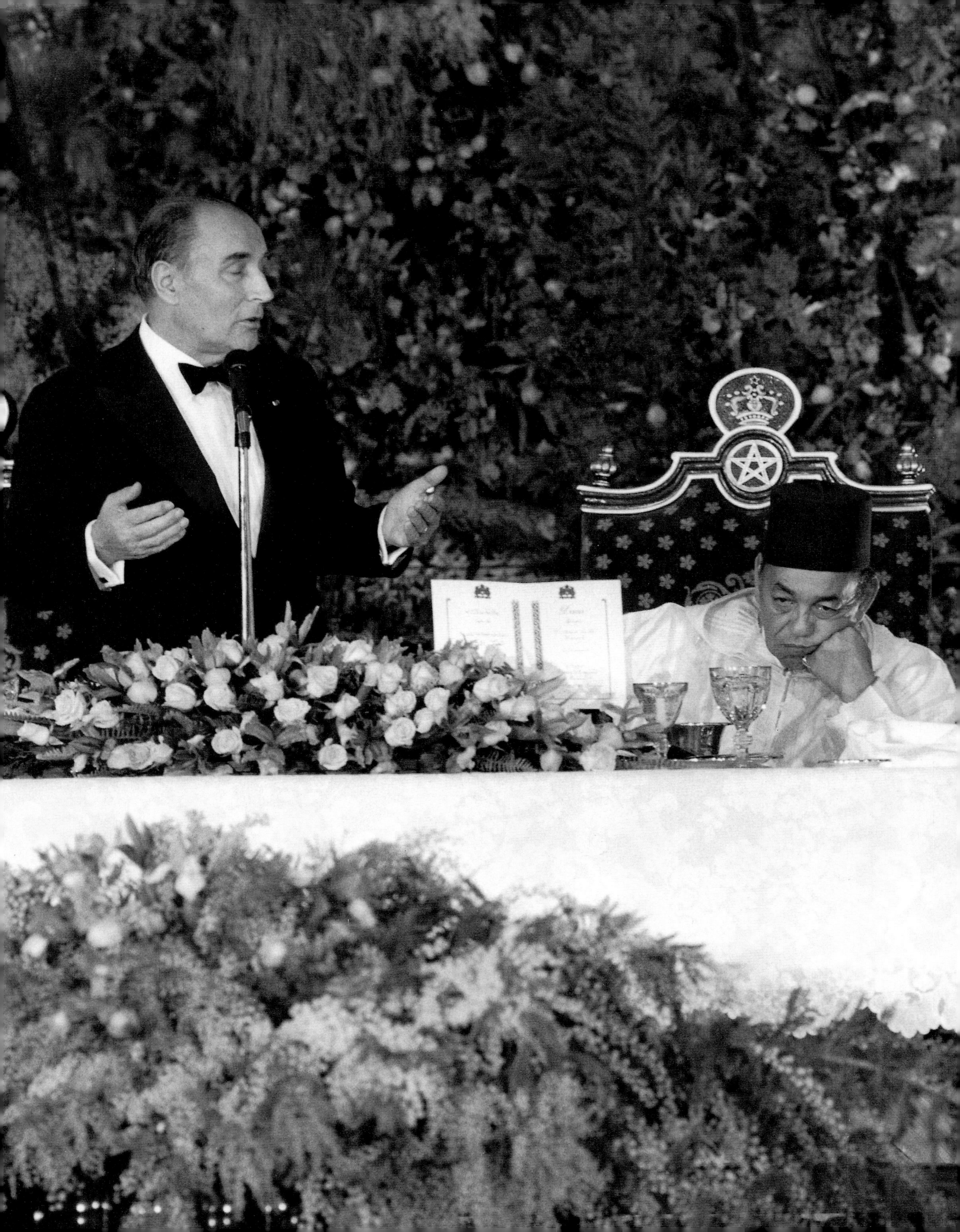

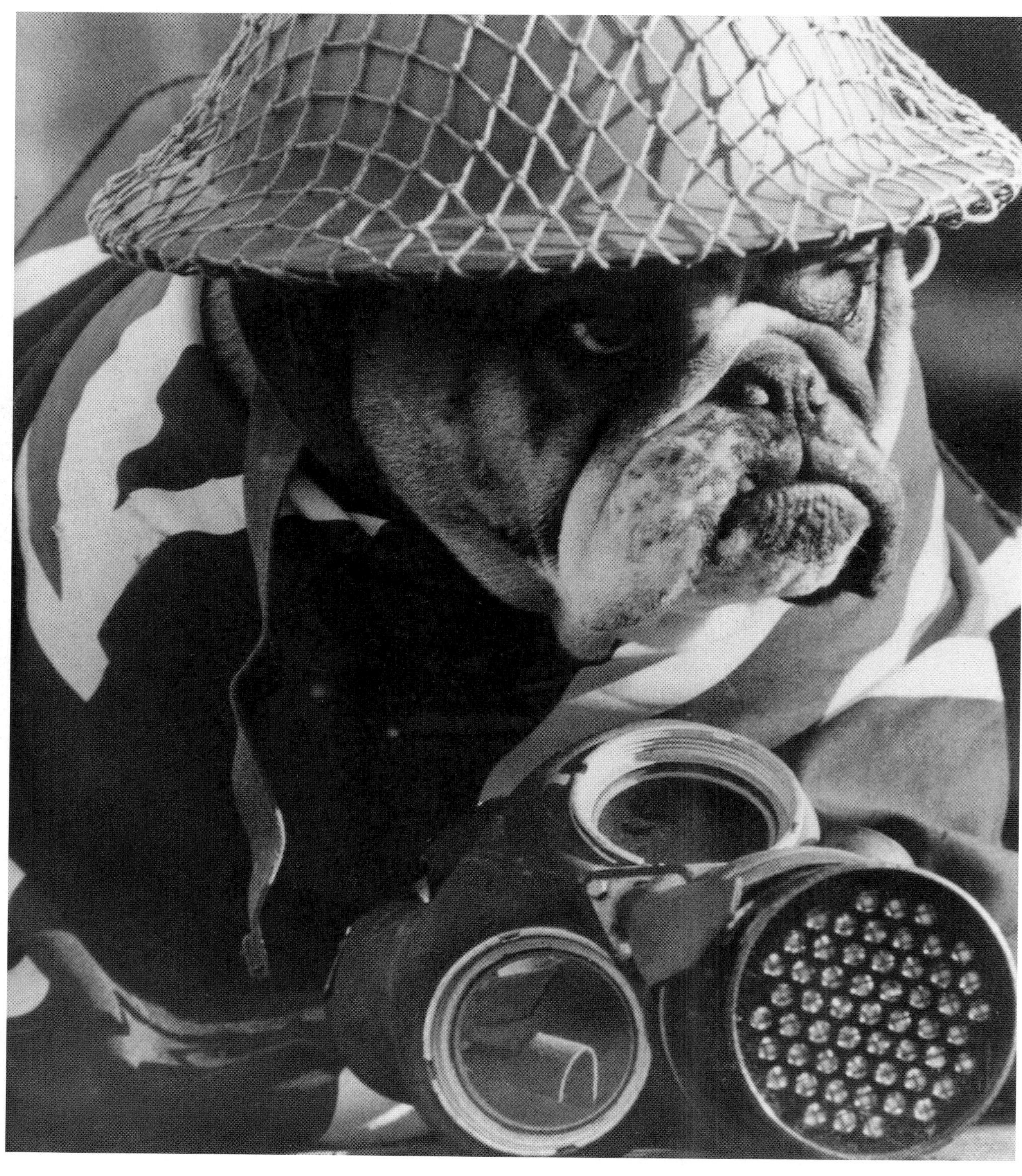

Commemoration of the Allied landing in Normandy
Only the cigar is missing . . . Winston the bulldog, star of the 50th anniversary commemoration.

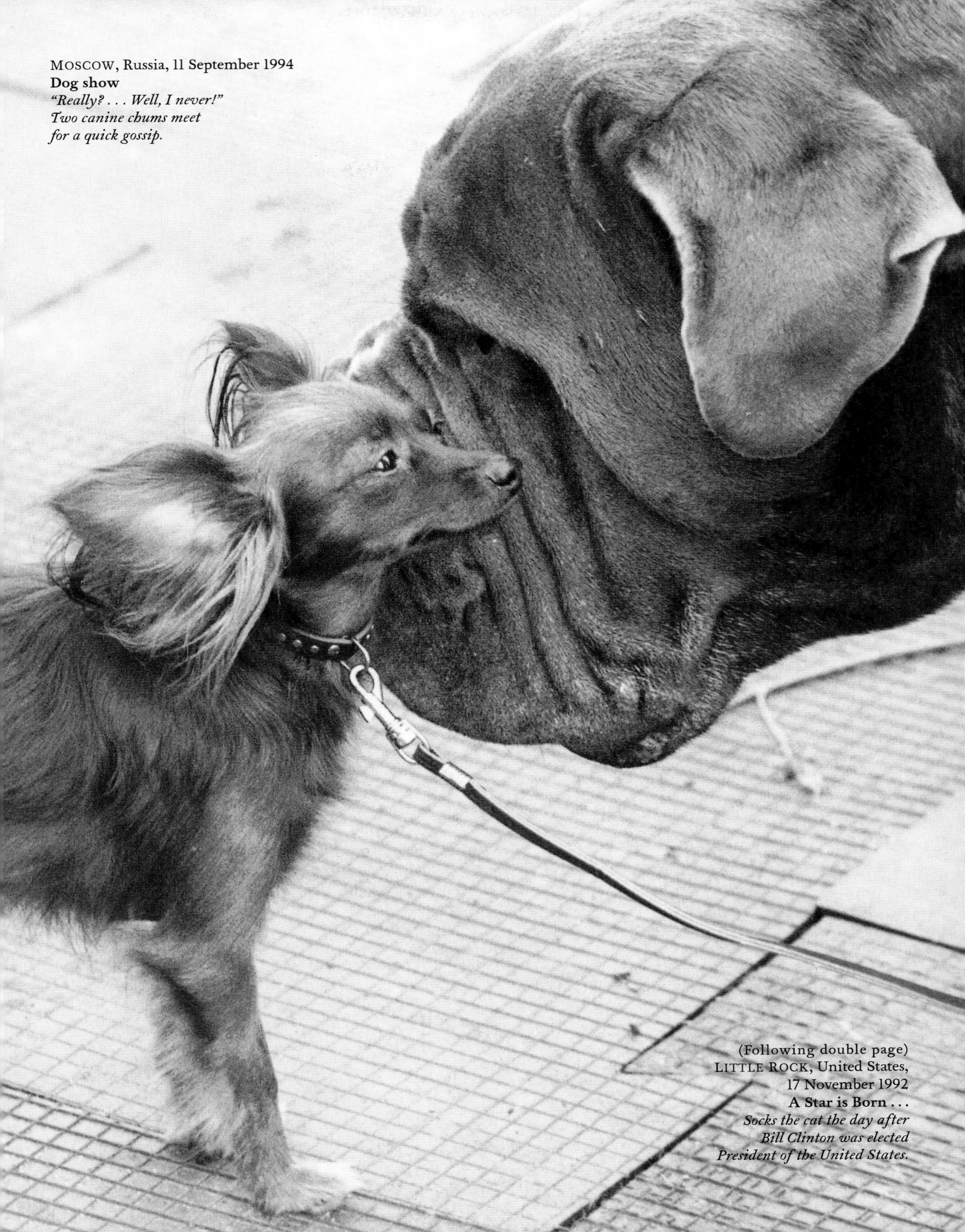

MOSCOW, Russia, 11 September 1994
Dog show
"Really? . . . Well, I never!"
Two canine chums meet
for a quick gossip.

(Following double page)
LITTLE ROCK, United States,
17 November 1992
A Star is Born . . .
Socks the cat the day after
Bill Clinton was elected
President of the United States.

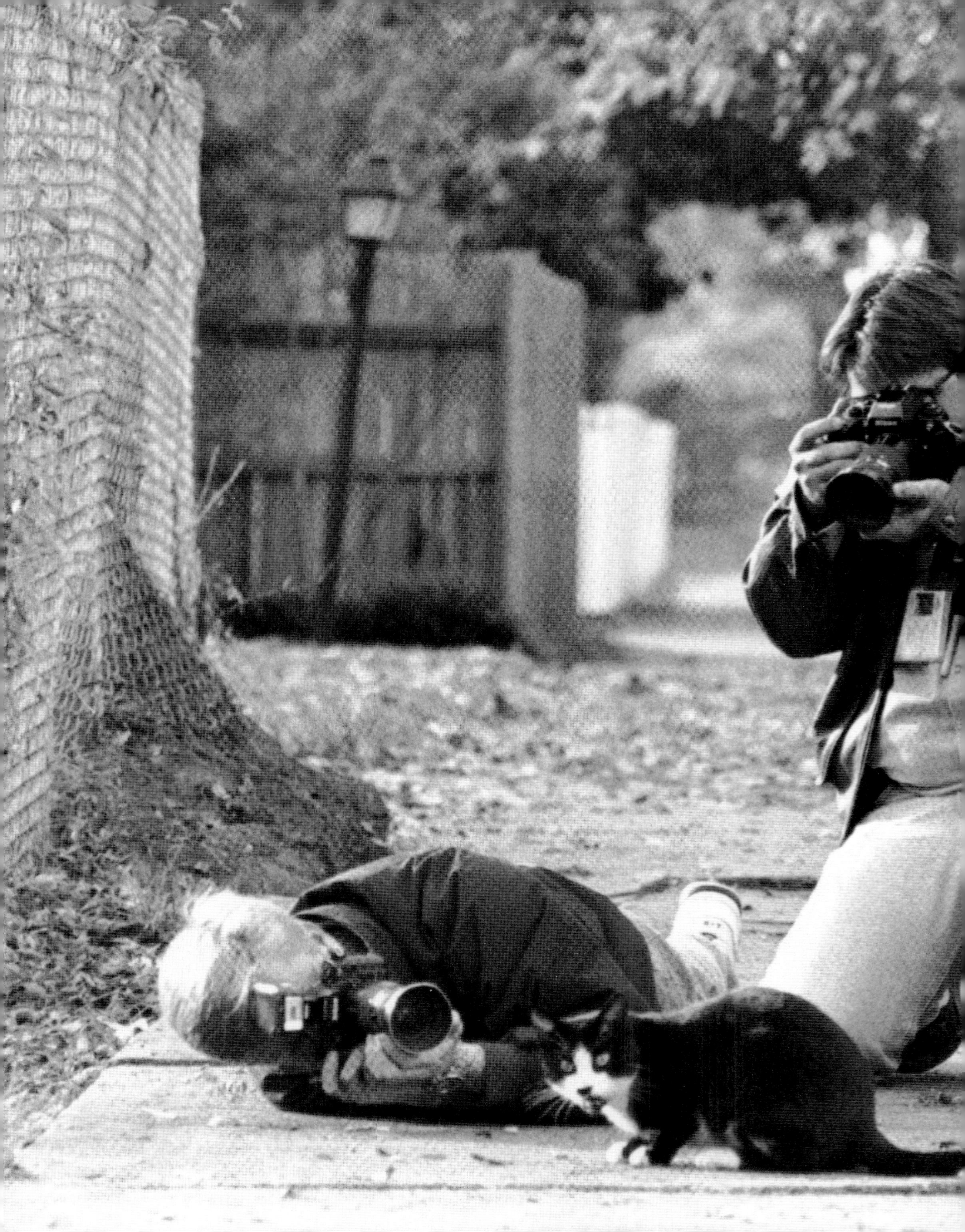

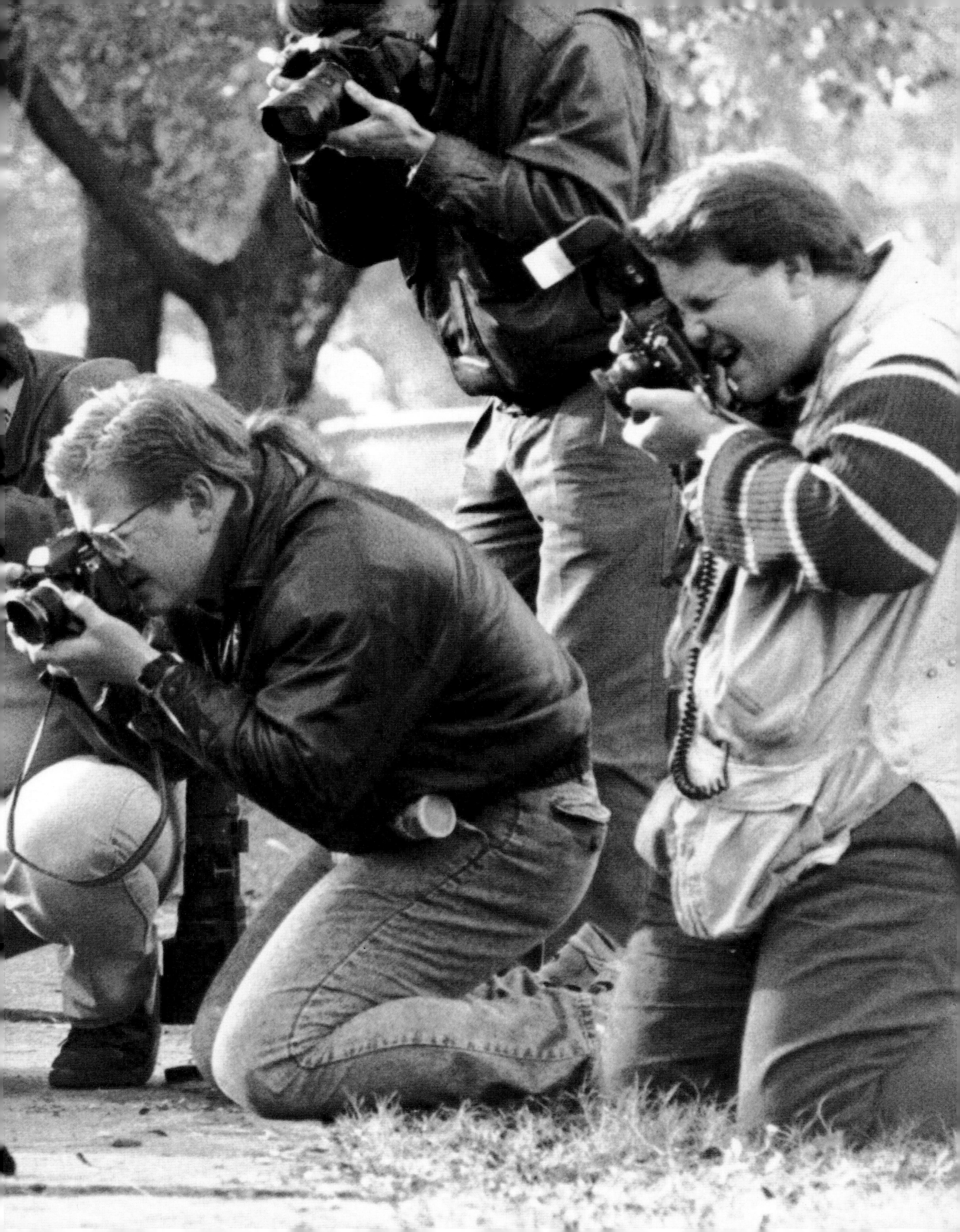

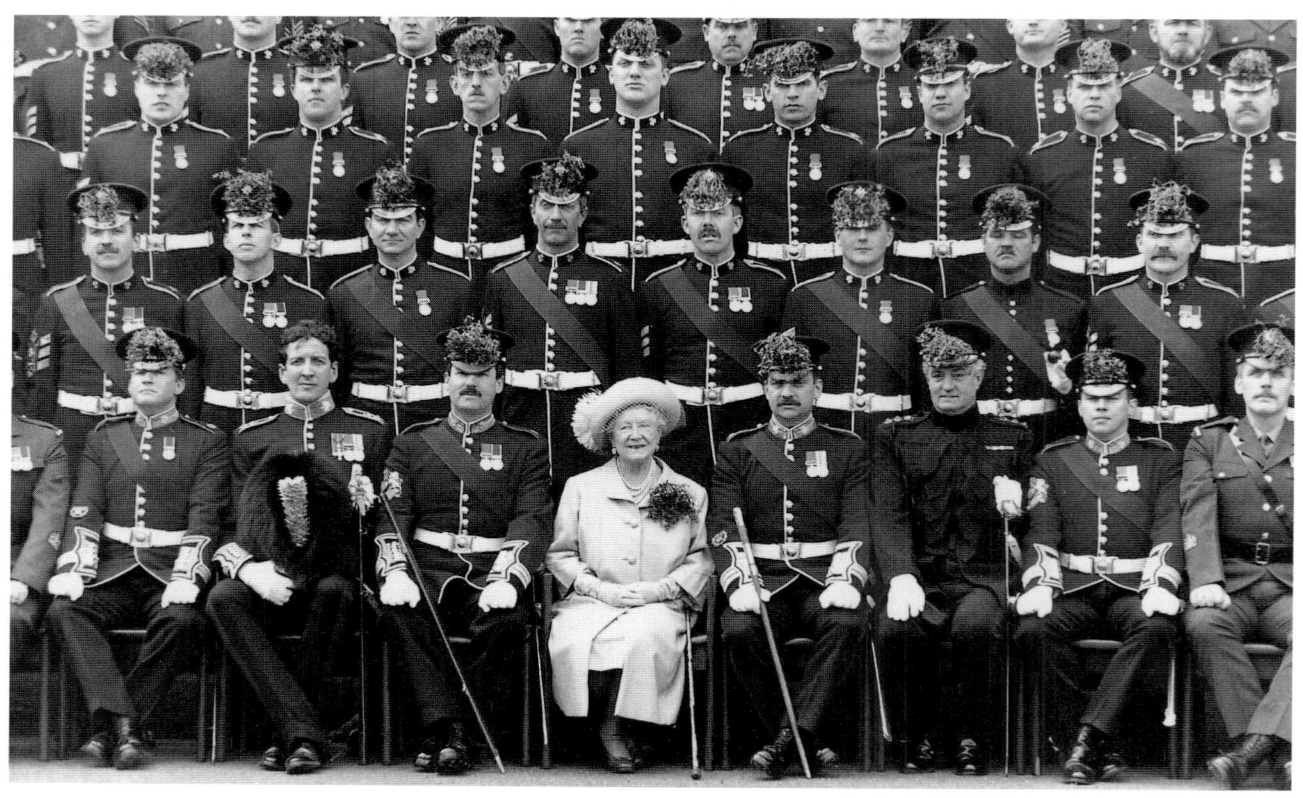

LONDON, Great Britain, 17 March 1994
Only the Queen Mother fails to keep a straight face at the headgear sported by the Irish Guards on St. Patrick's Day.

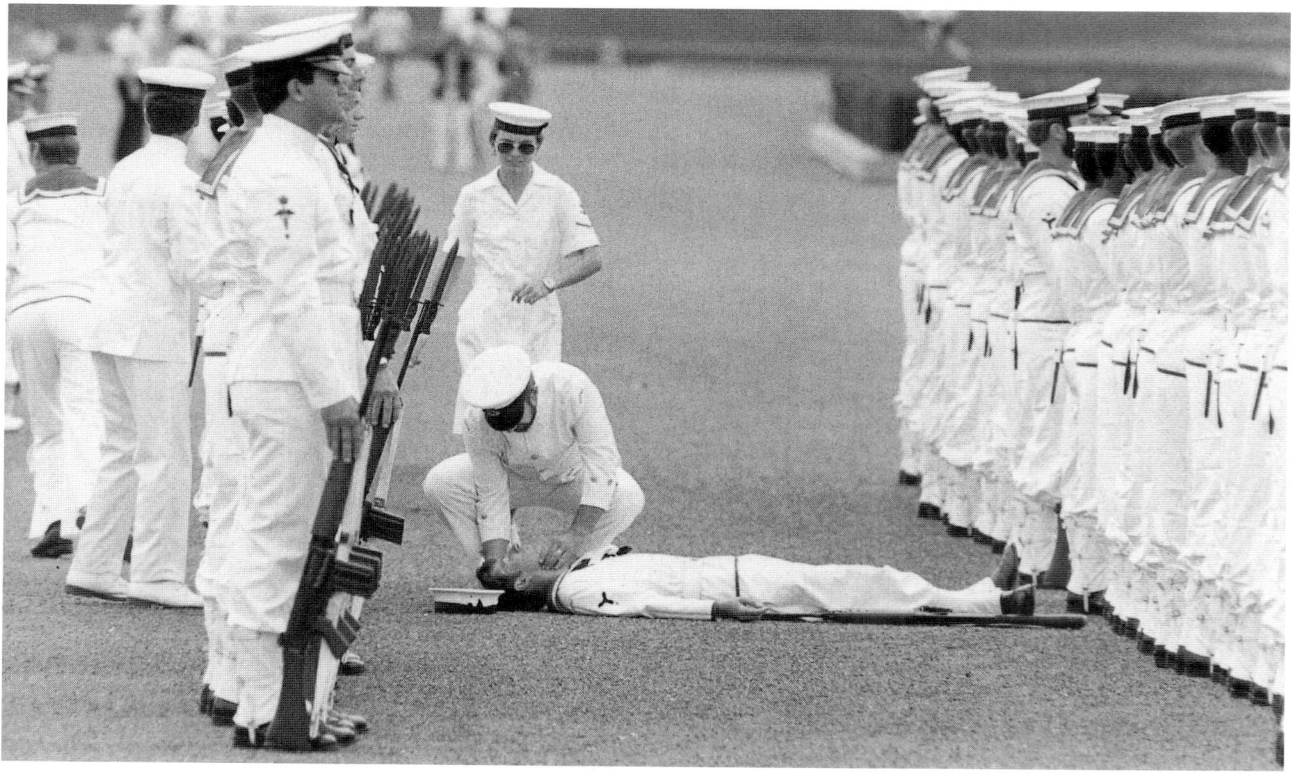

CANBERRA, Australia, 3 March 1986
Whether it is emotion at the passage of Queen Elizabeth II or a simple case of sunstroke, this naval cadet is out for the count.

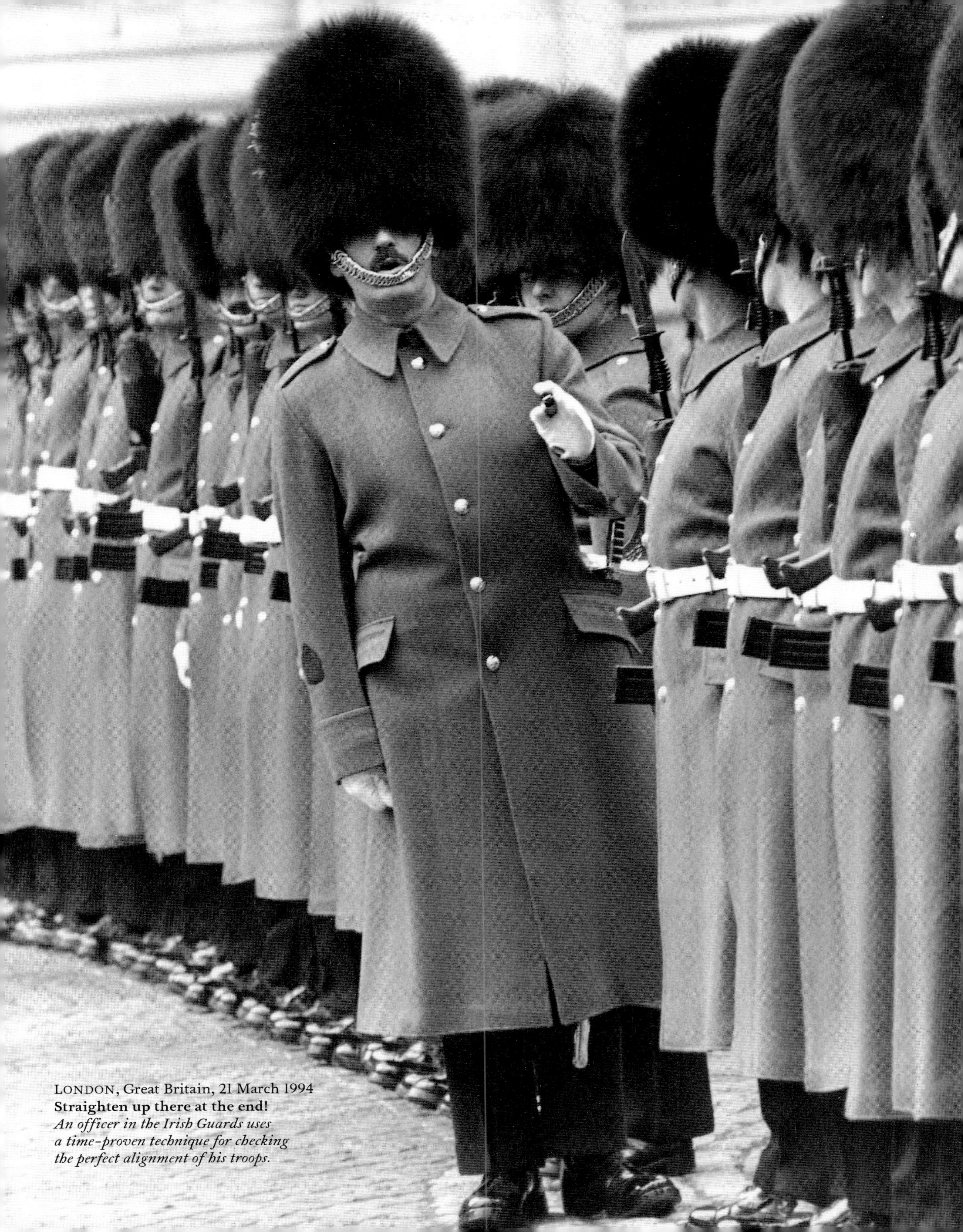

LONDON, Great Britain, 21 March 1994
Straighten up there at the end!
*An officer in the Irish Guards uses
a time-proven technique for checking
the perfect alignment of his troops.*

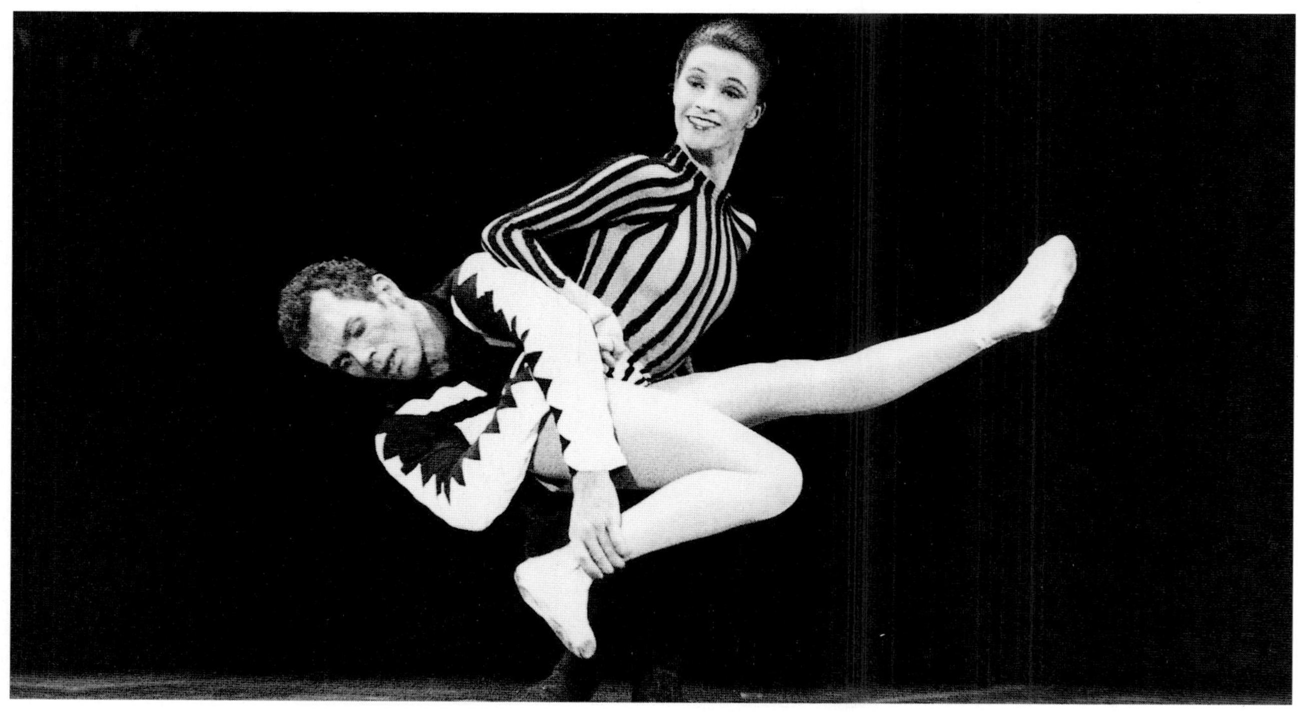

PARIS, France, 8 March 1994
Rehearsal of Roland Petit's ballet Waltz Rhythm. *Is that my leg or yours?*

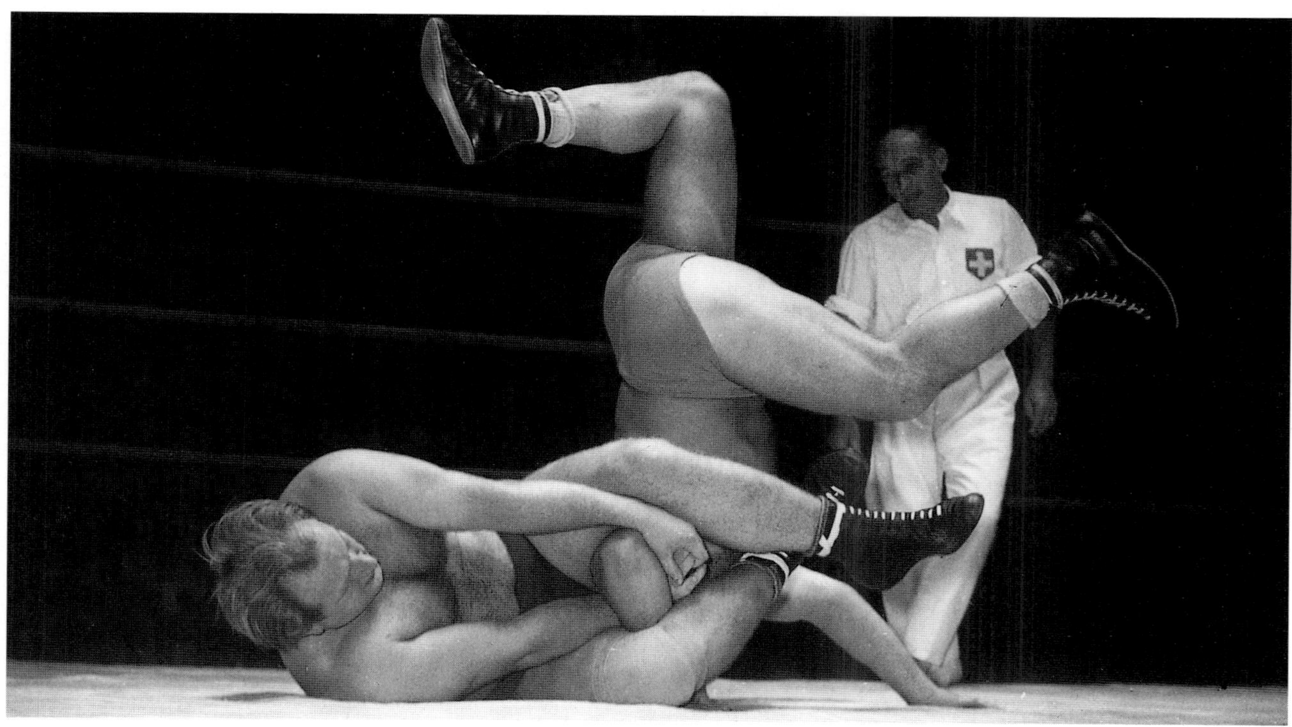

KARLSRUHE, Germany, 27 April 1955
World Wrestling Championships. *Tied up in knots . . .*

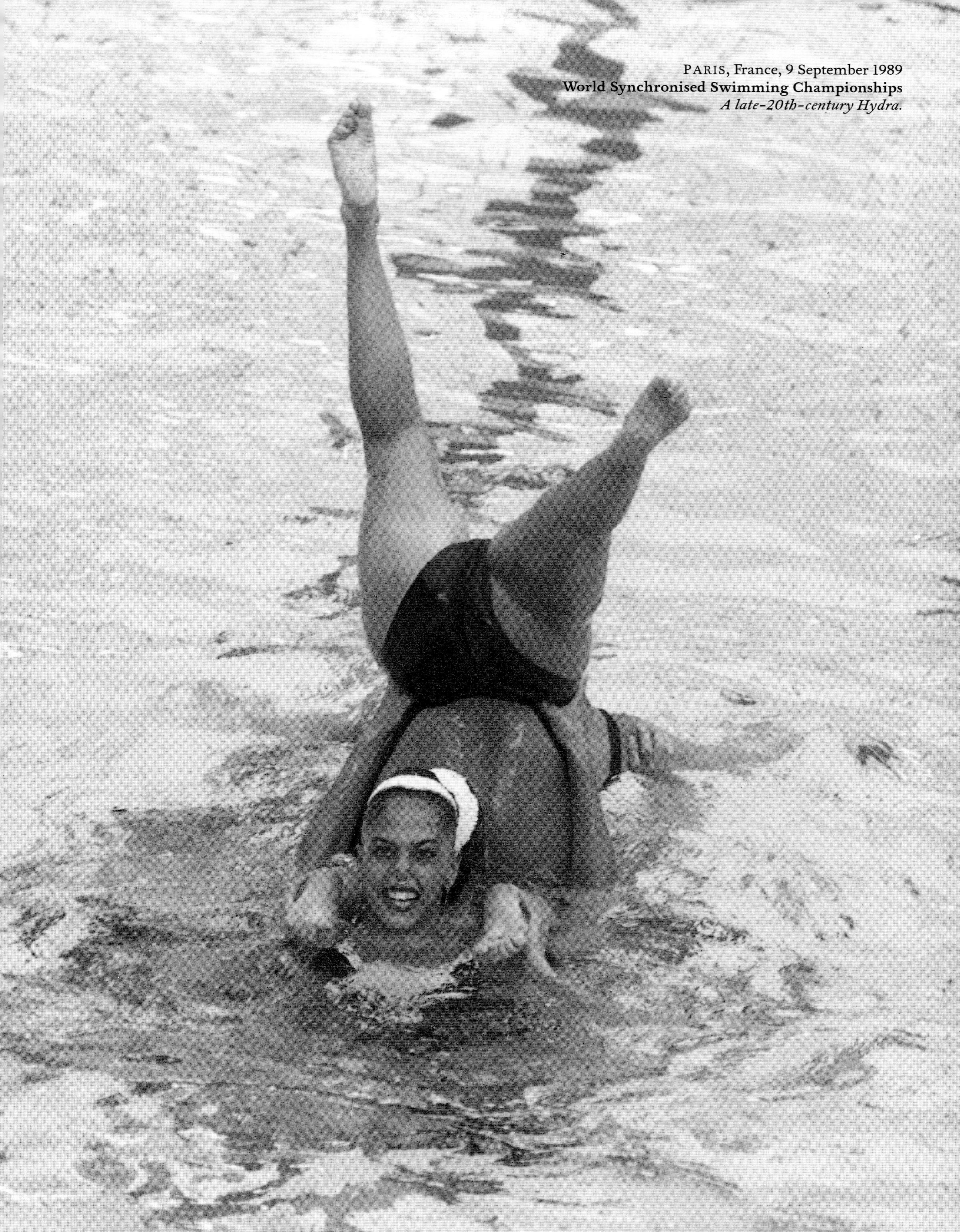

PARIS, France, 9 September 1989
World Synchronised Swimming Championships
A late-20th-century Hydra.

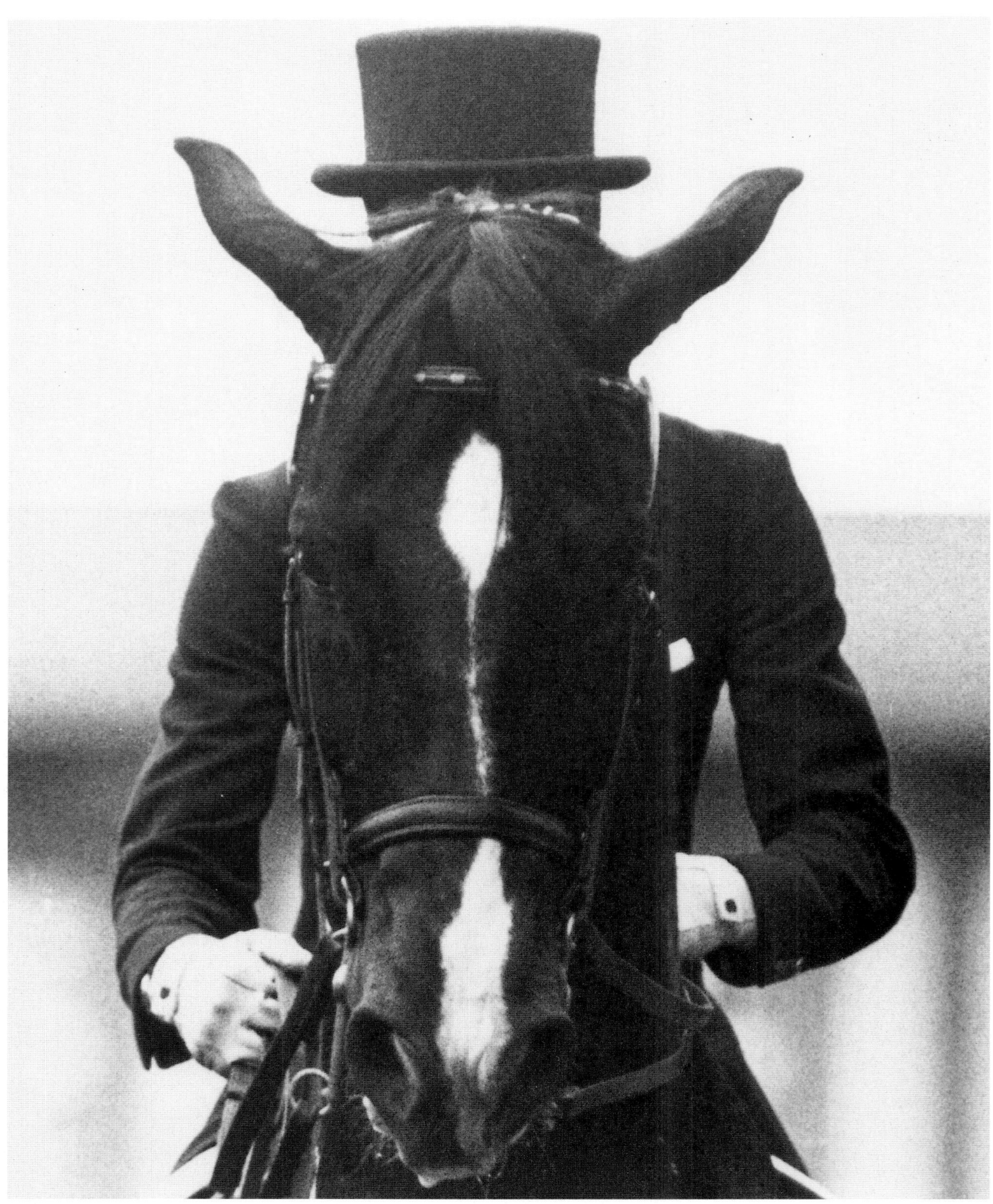

WIESBADEN, Germany, 20 May 1991
Equestrian competition
Hats off to this horse, who won.

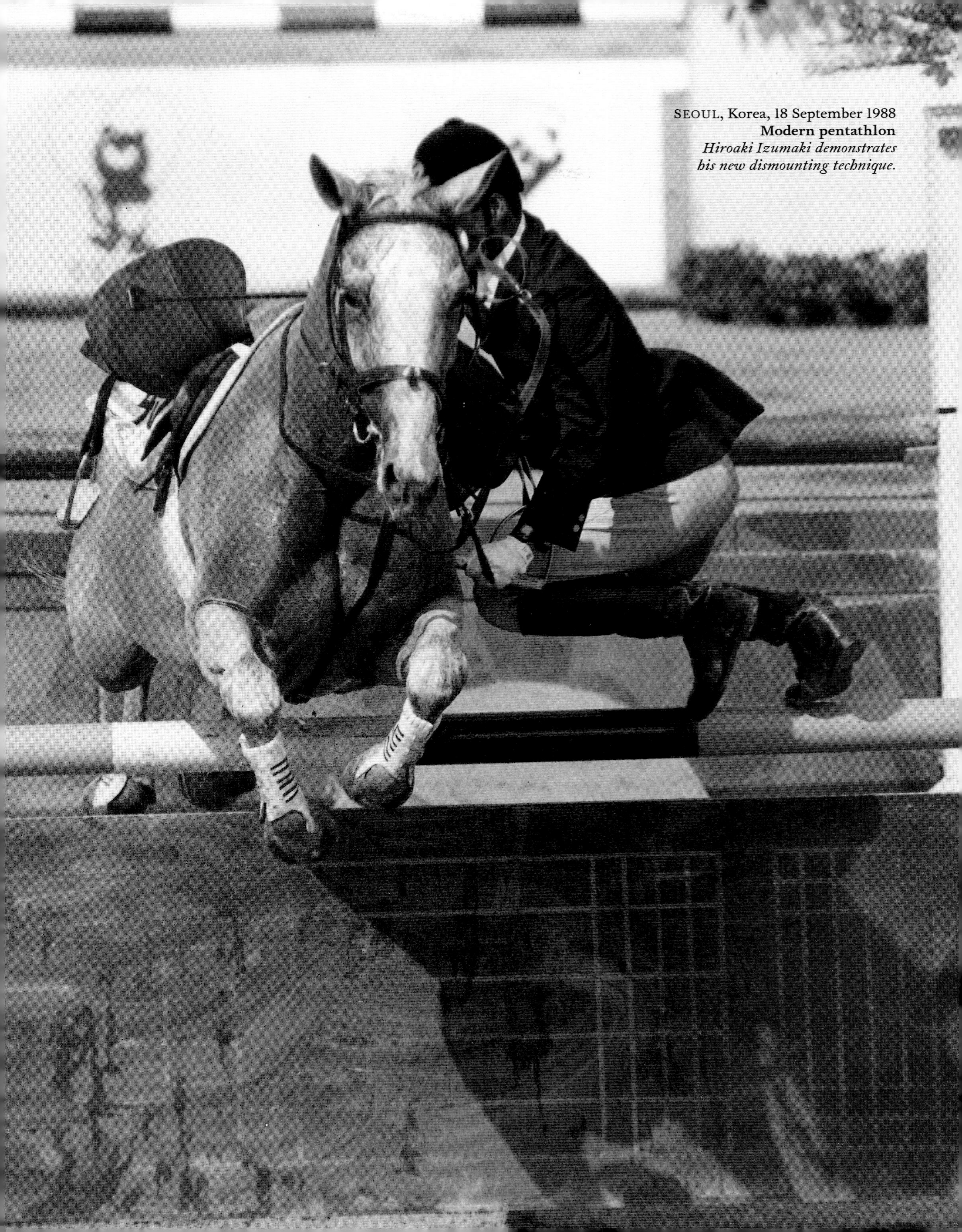

SEOUL, Korea, 18 September 1988
Modern pentathlon
Hiroaki Izumaki demonstrates
his new dismounting technique.

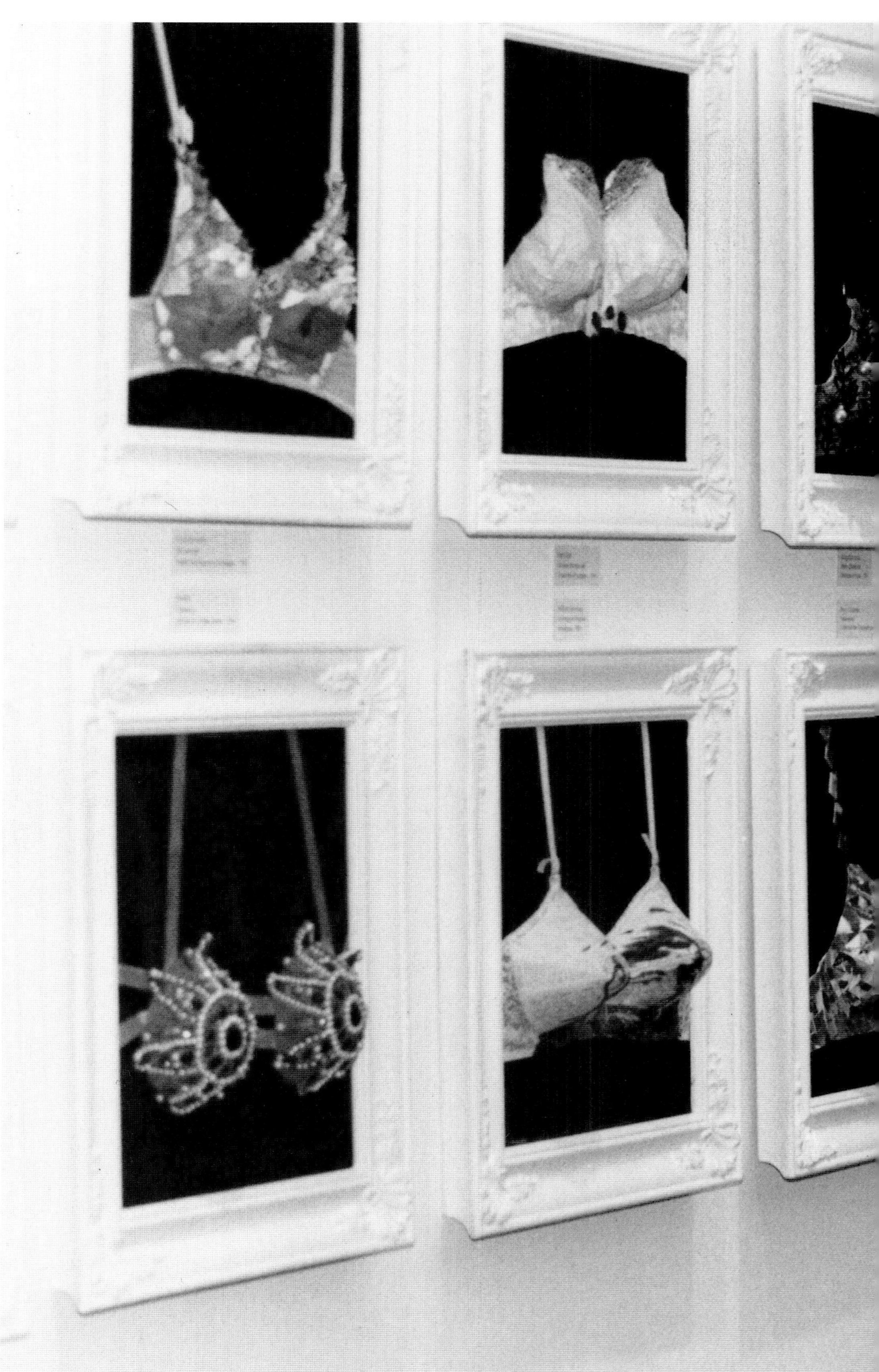

PARIS, France,
11 August 1994
**Exhibition of bras
from the collection of
Samuele Mazza**
*On closer inspection . . .
One art aficionado tries
to get a more intimate
perspective.*

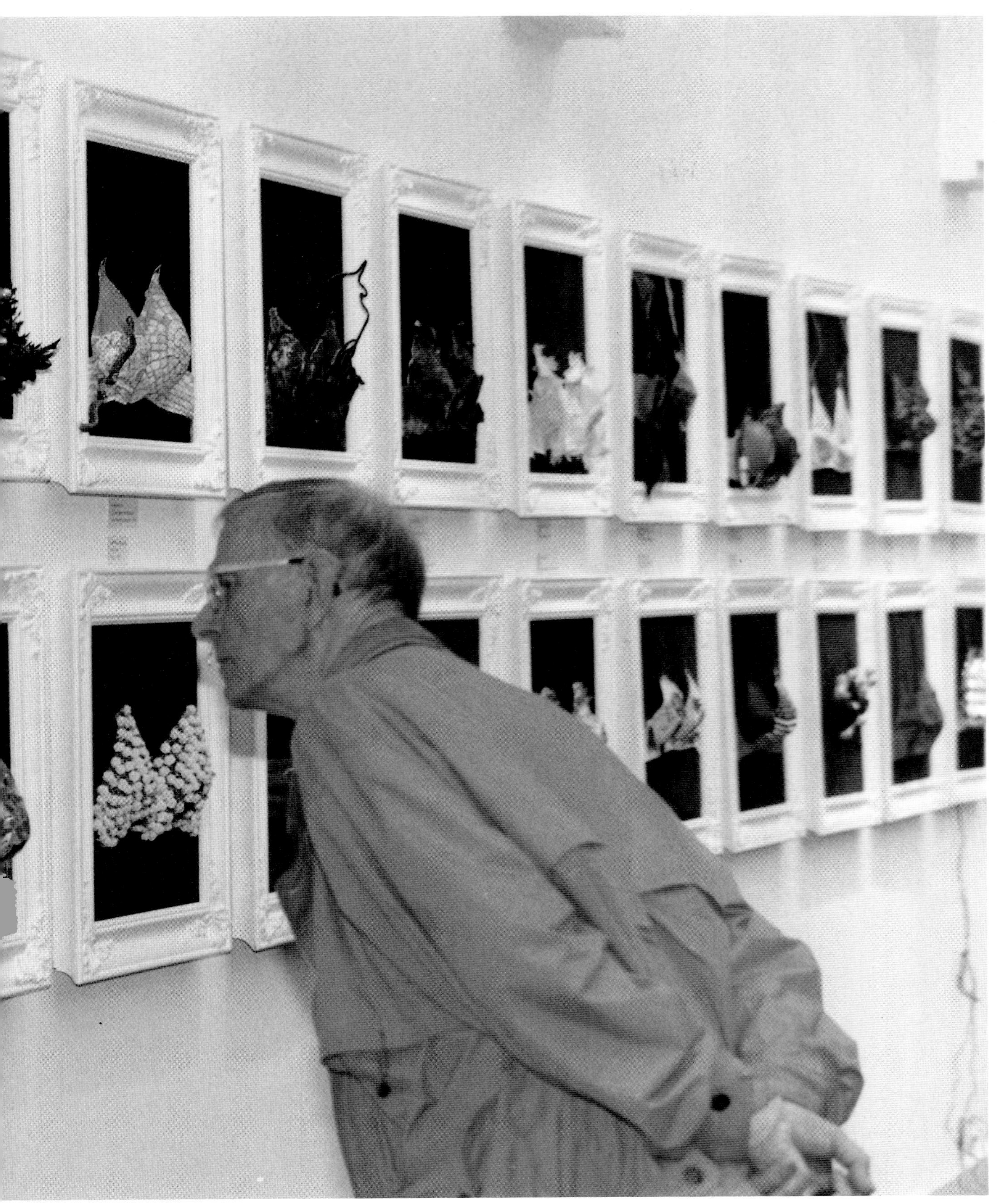

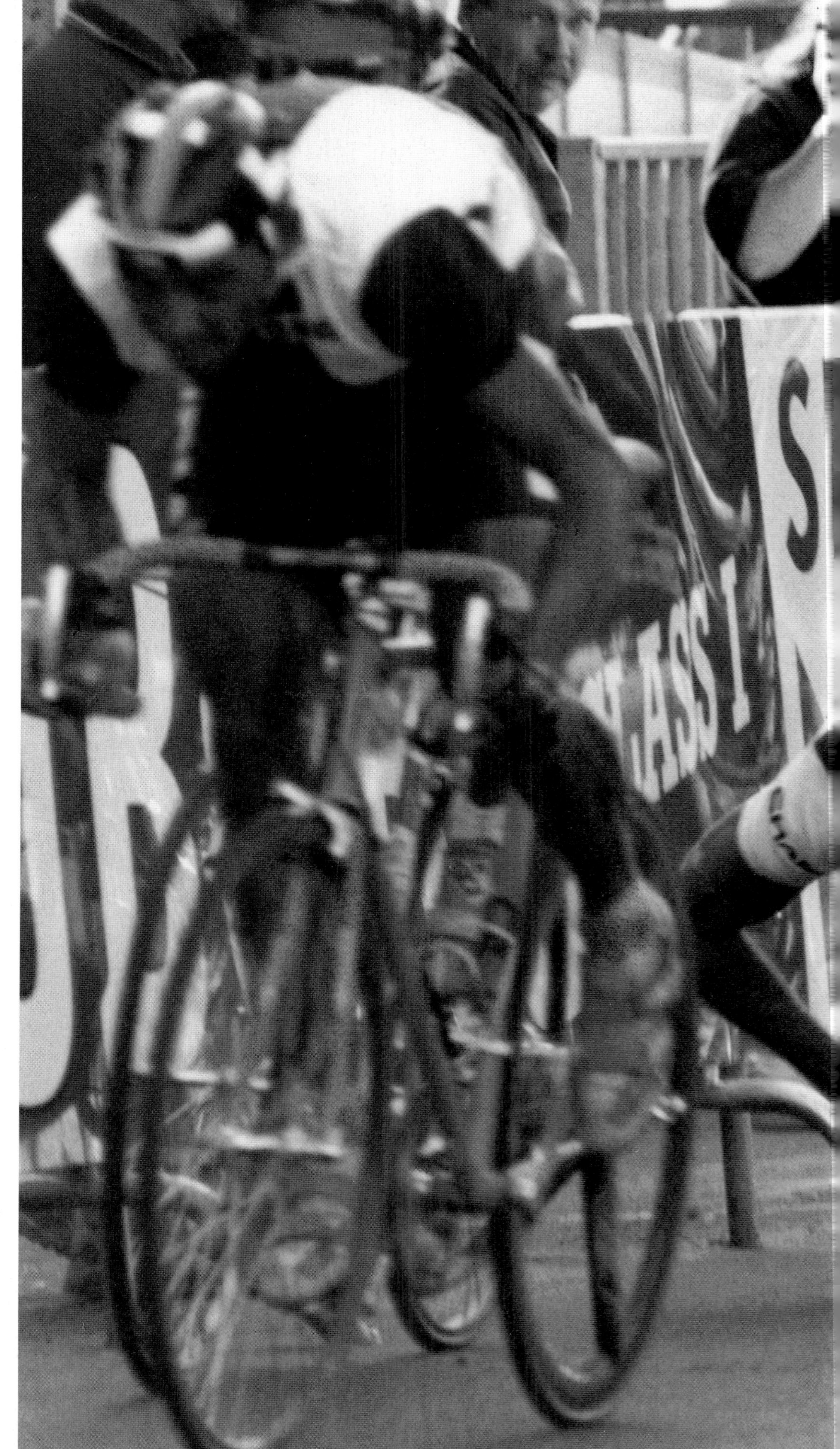

OSLO, Norway,
28 August 1993
**World Amateur Cycling
Championships**
*A Danish cyclist goes for
the photo finish . . .*

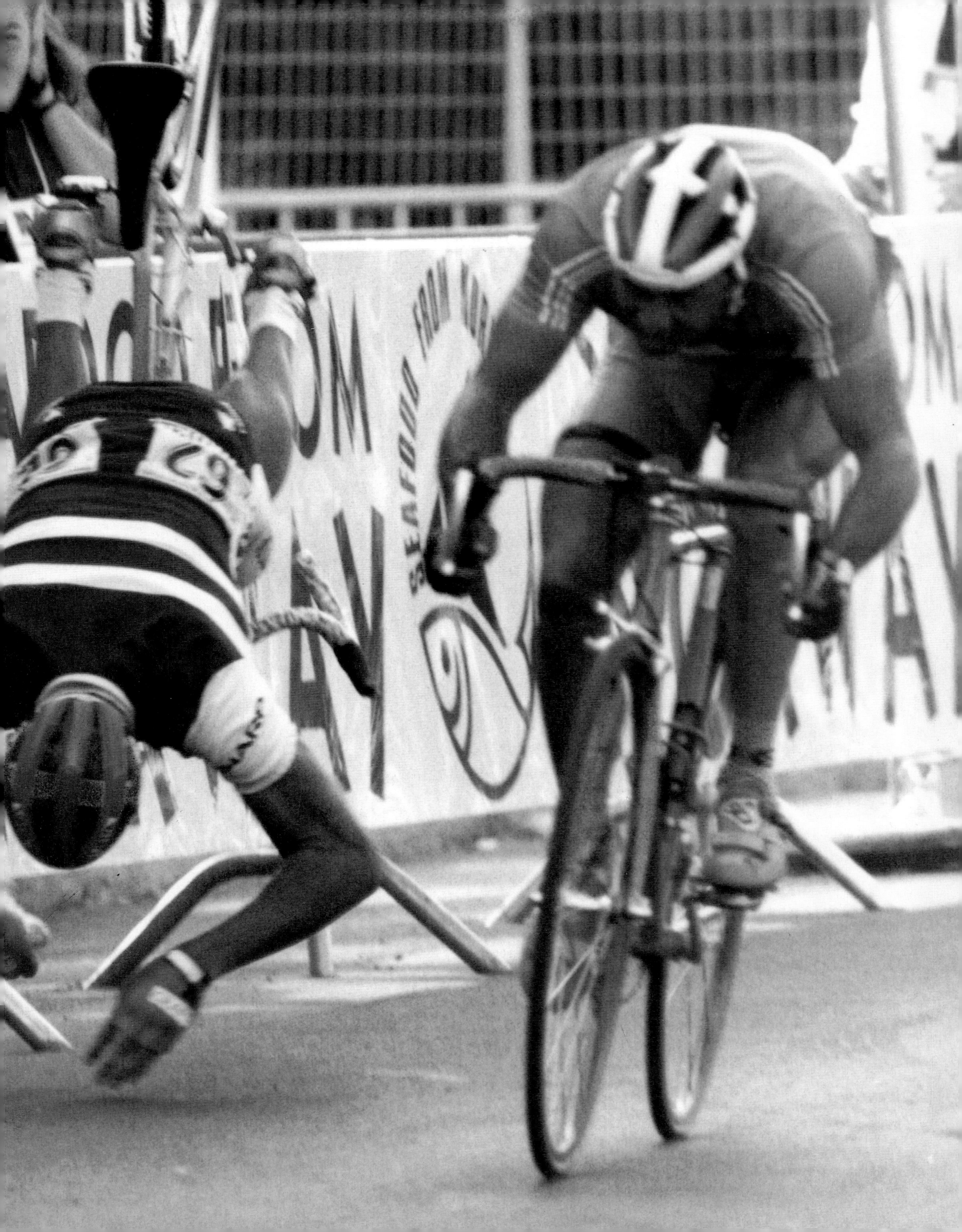

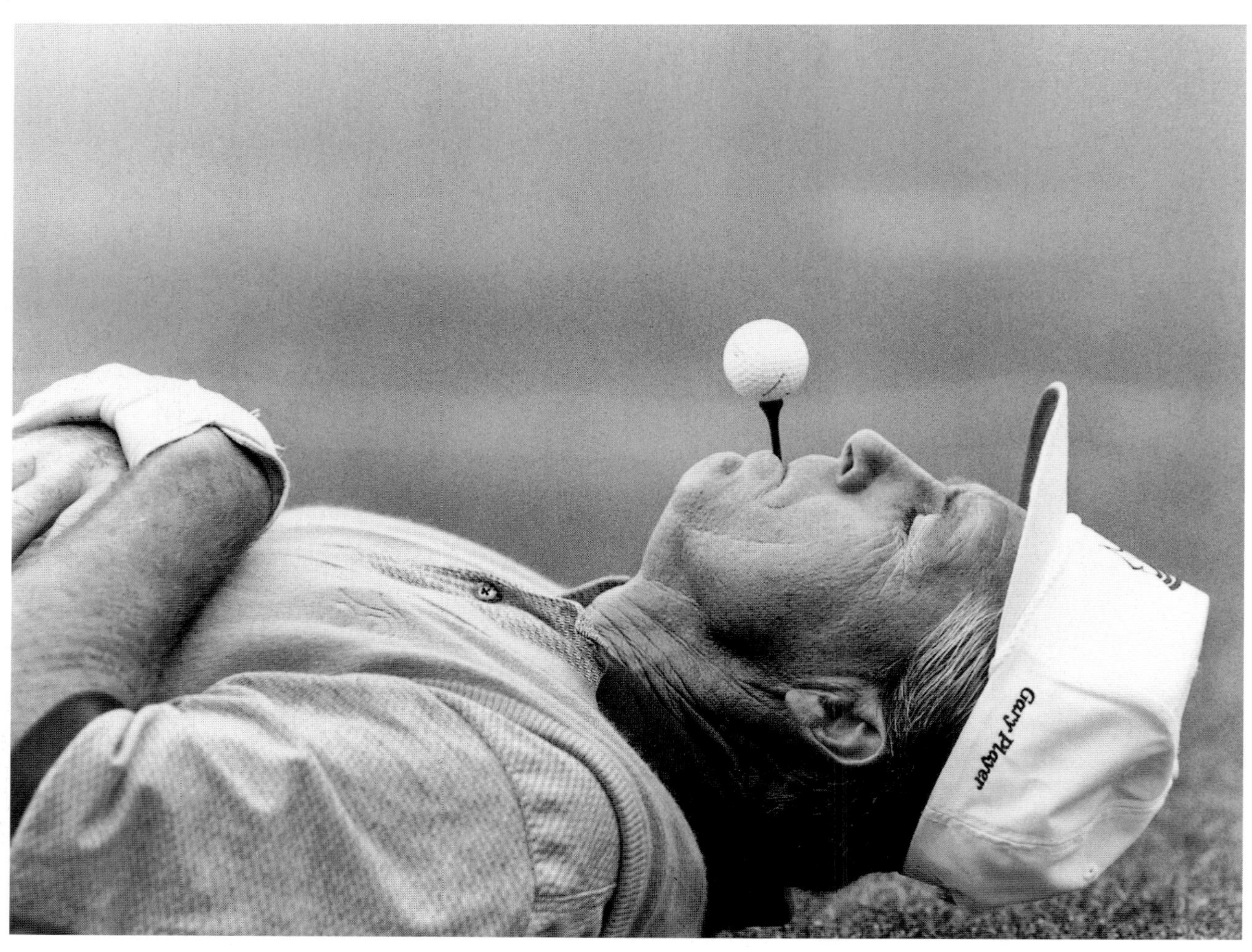

MARYLAND, United States, 28 June 1995
British golfer Gary Player *exhibits a stiff upper lip
at the United States Open Championship.*

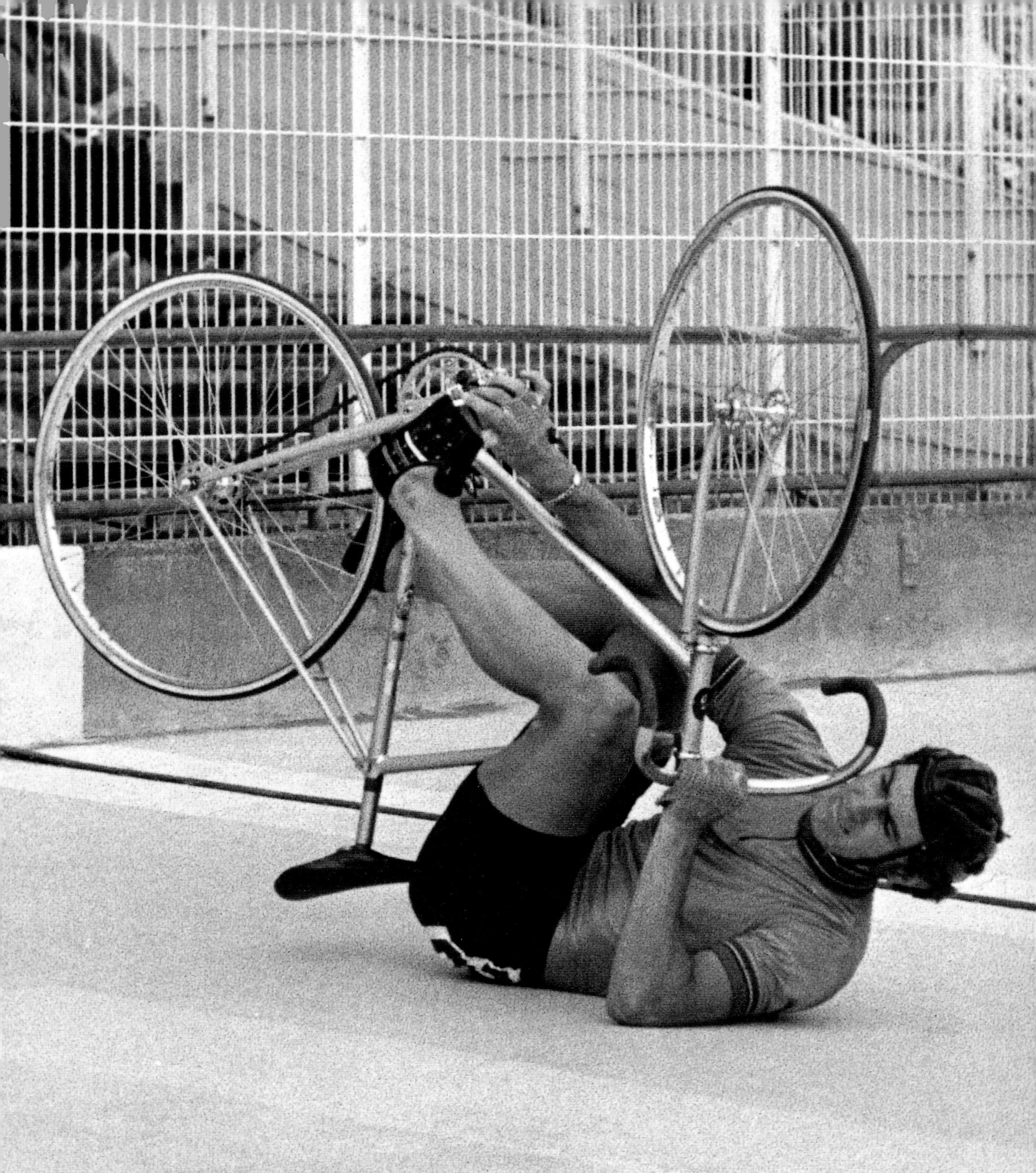

LIEGE, Belgium, 22 August 1975
Once over the finishing line, *a rider and his bicycle have troubling separating.*

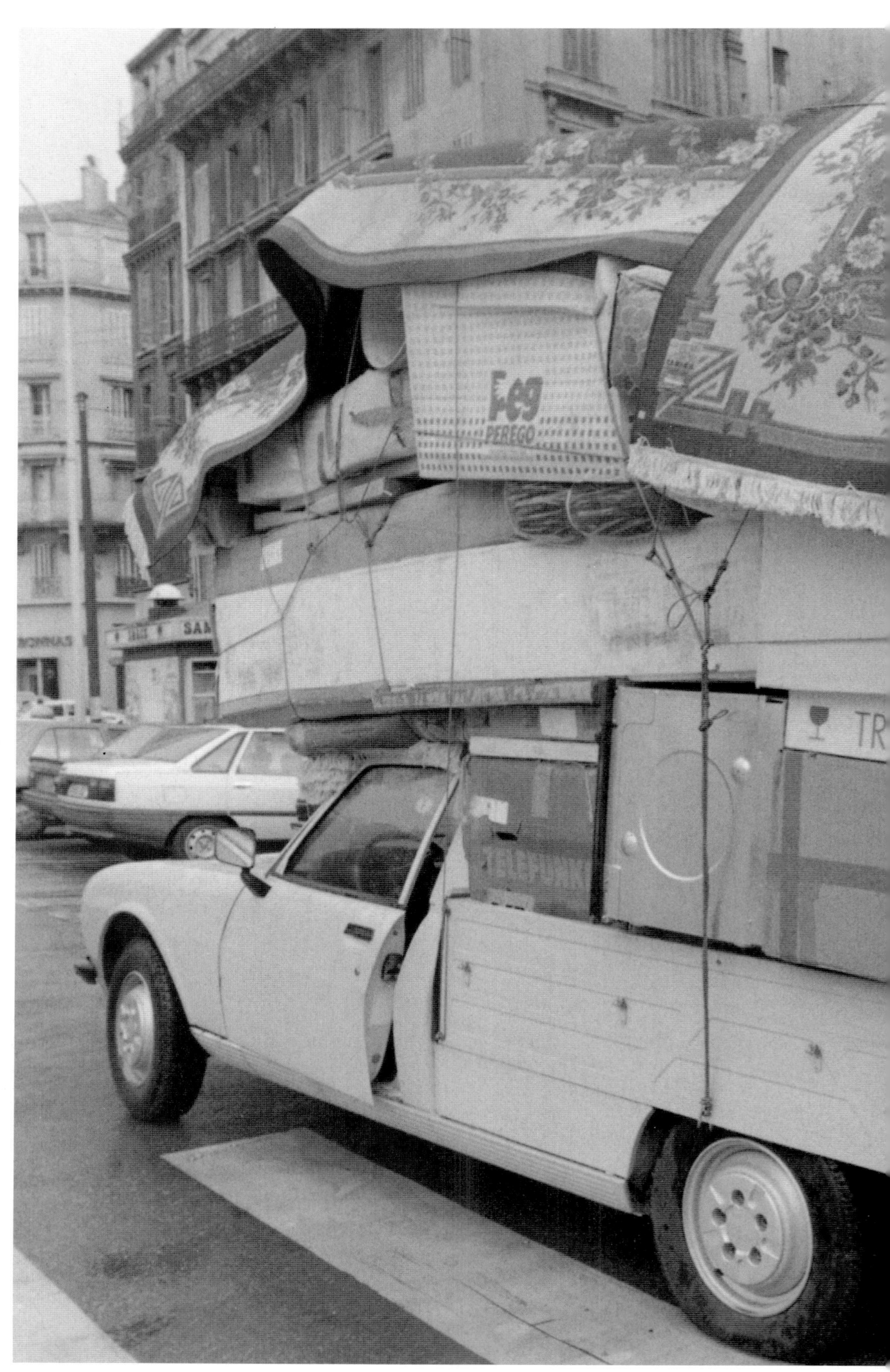

MARSEILLE, France,
15 October 1991
**Everything but
the kitchen sink . . .**

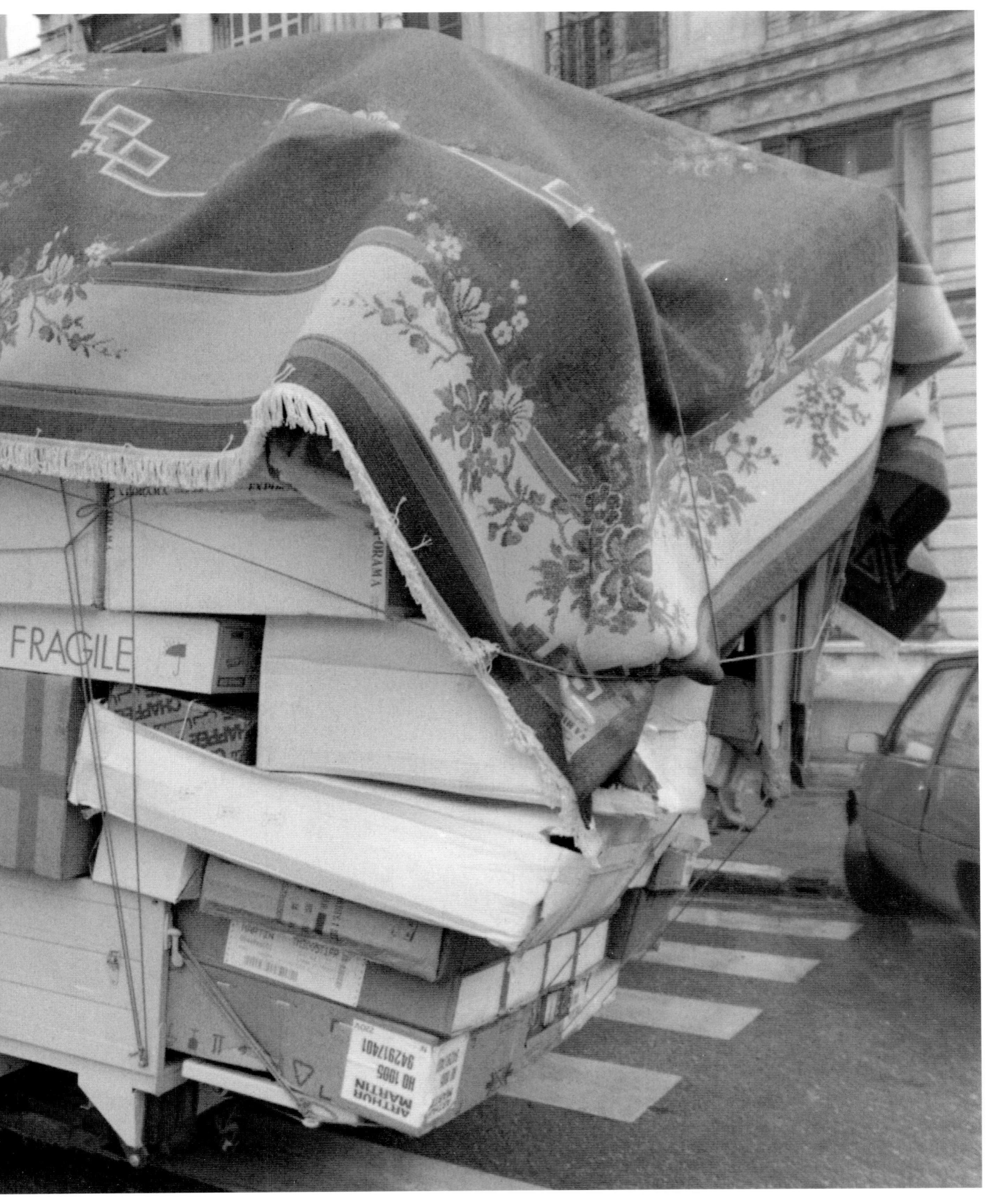

FRAGILE
ARTHUR MARTIN
NO 1905
9A2917401

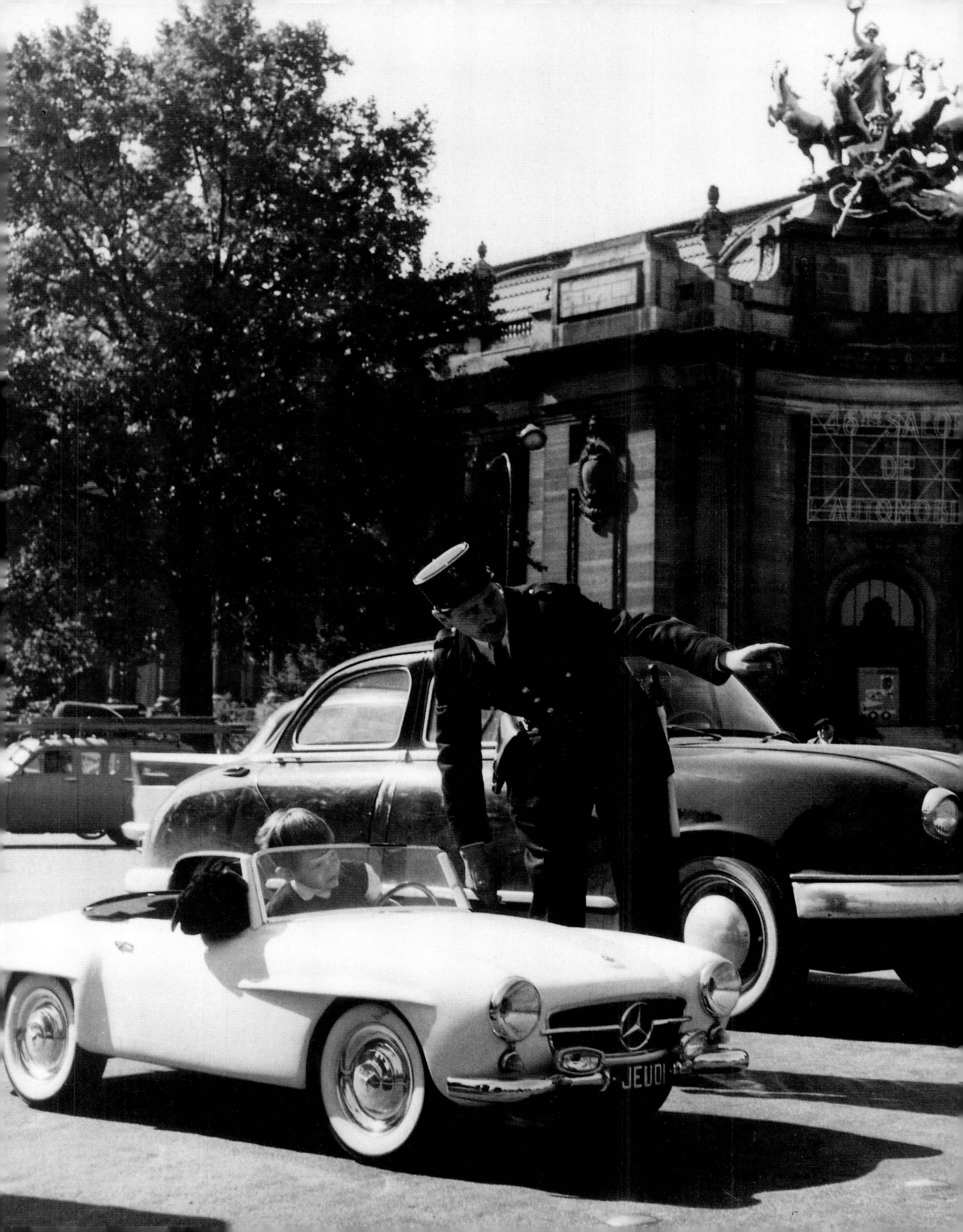

SALON
DE
L'AUTOMOBILE
JEUDI

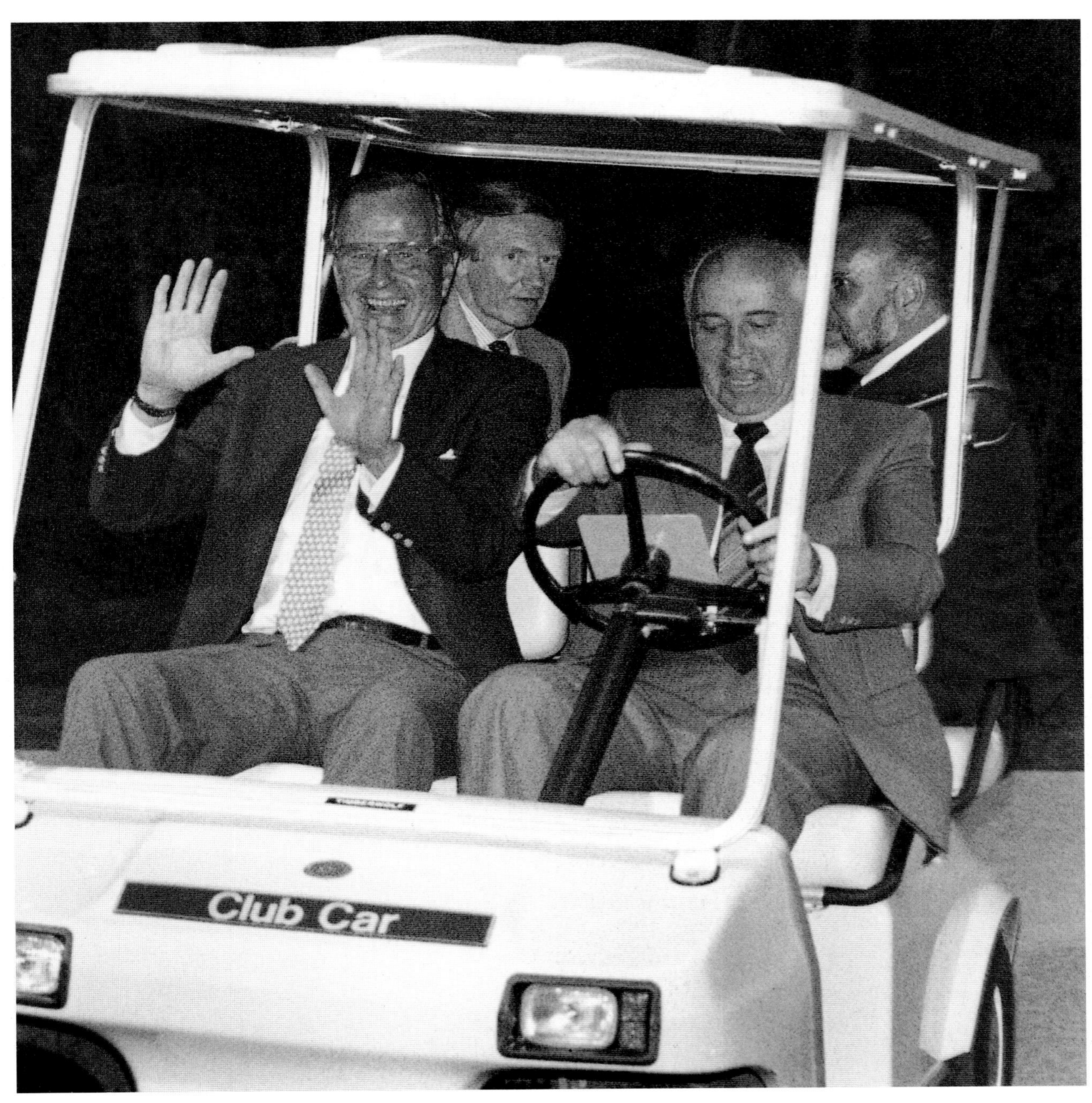

CAMP DAVID, Maryland, United States, 2 June 1990
Russia encounters a few problems
following the American path to democracy.

PARIS, France
Opening of the Motor Show
First on the left, sir.

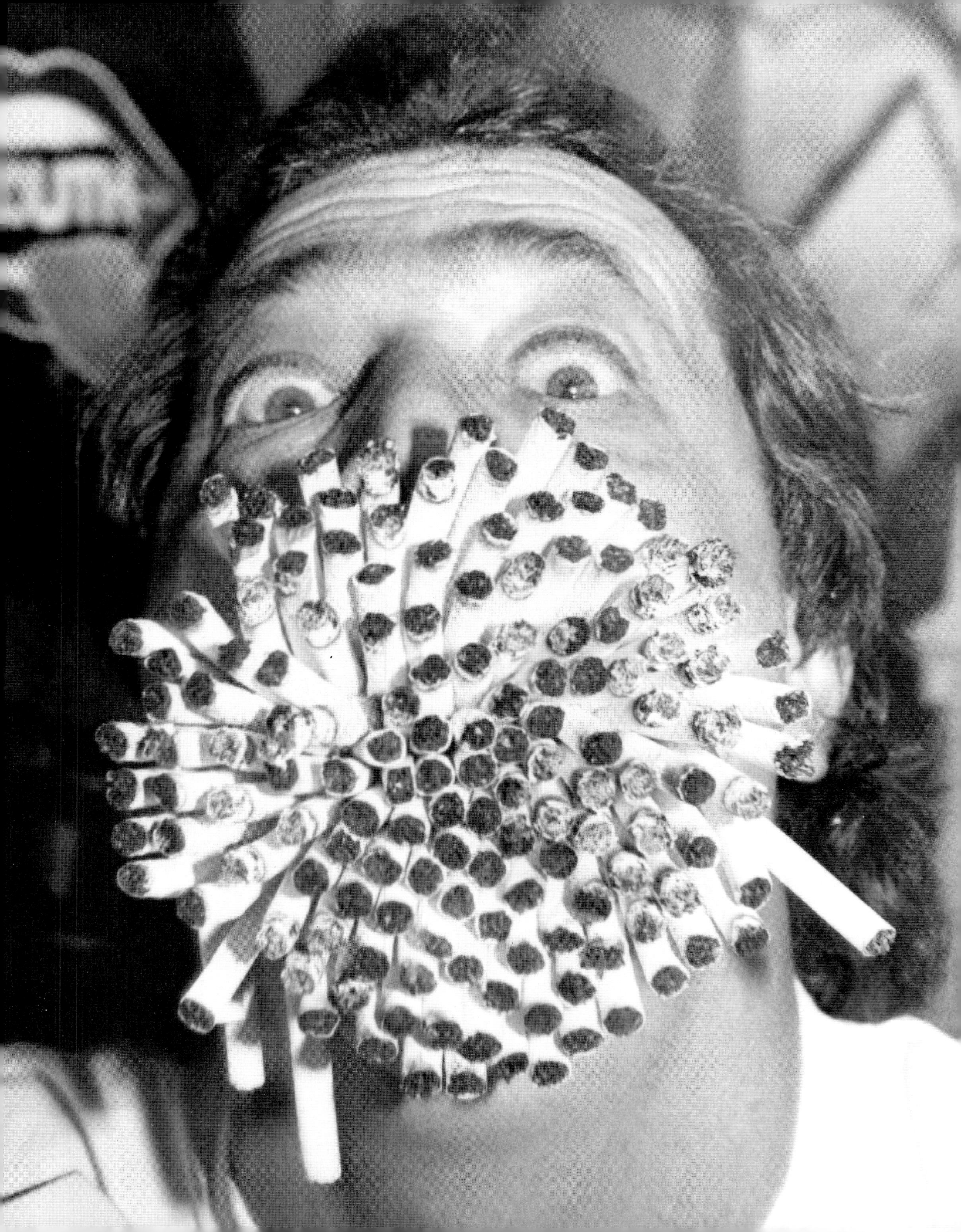

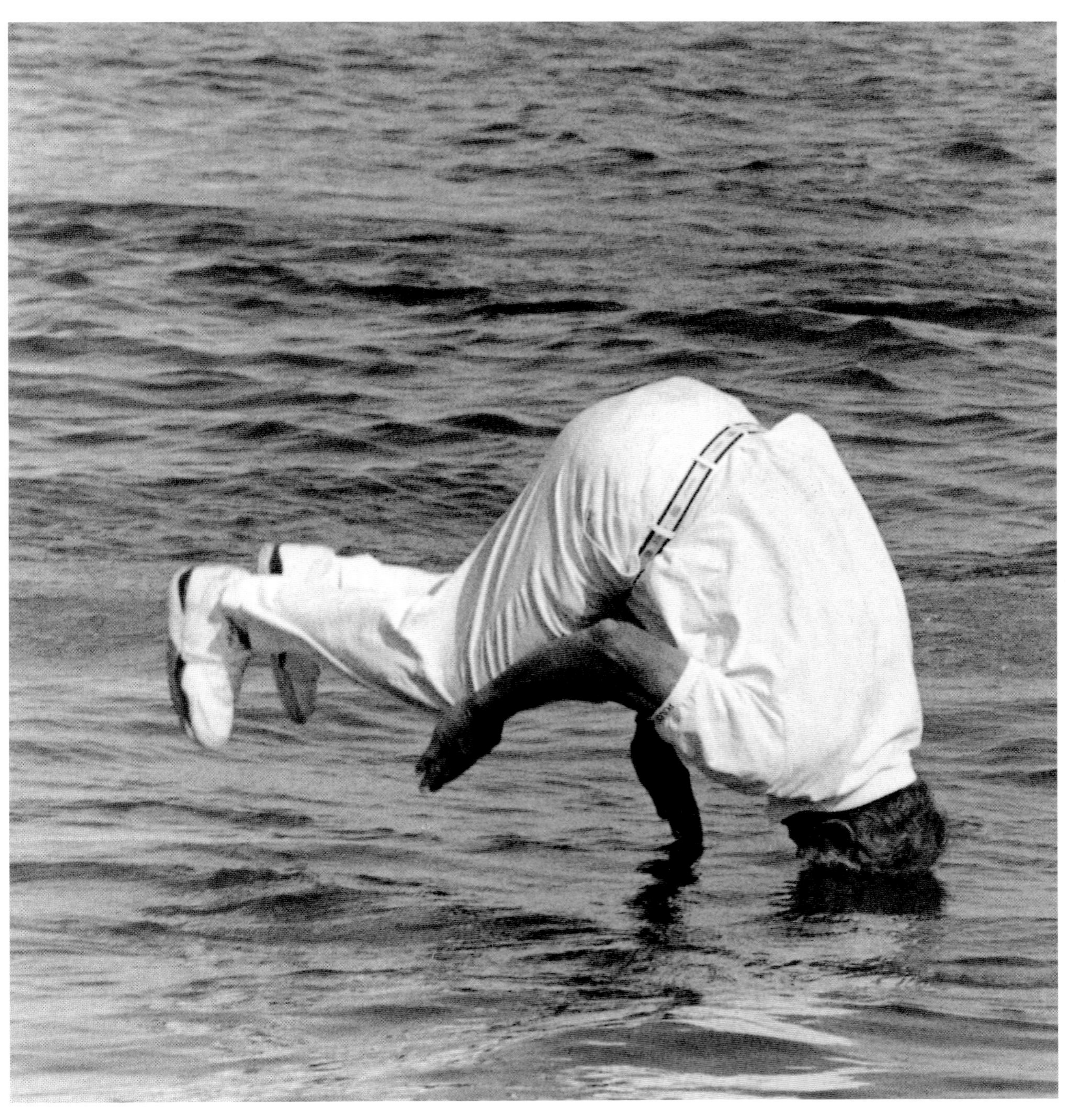

HOLLYWOOD, United States, 19 November 1992
Going up in smoke!
*The aptly named Jim "Mouth" smokes 154 cigarettes at once
to win a place in the* Guiness Book of Records.

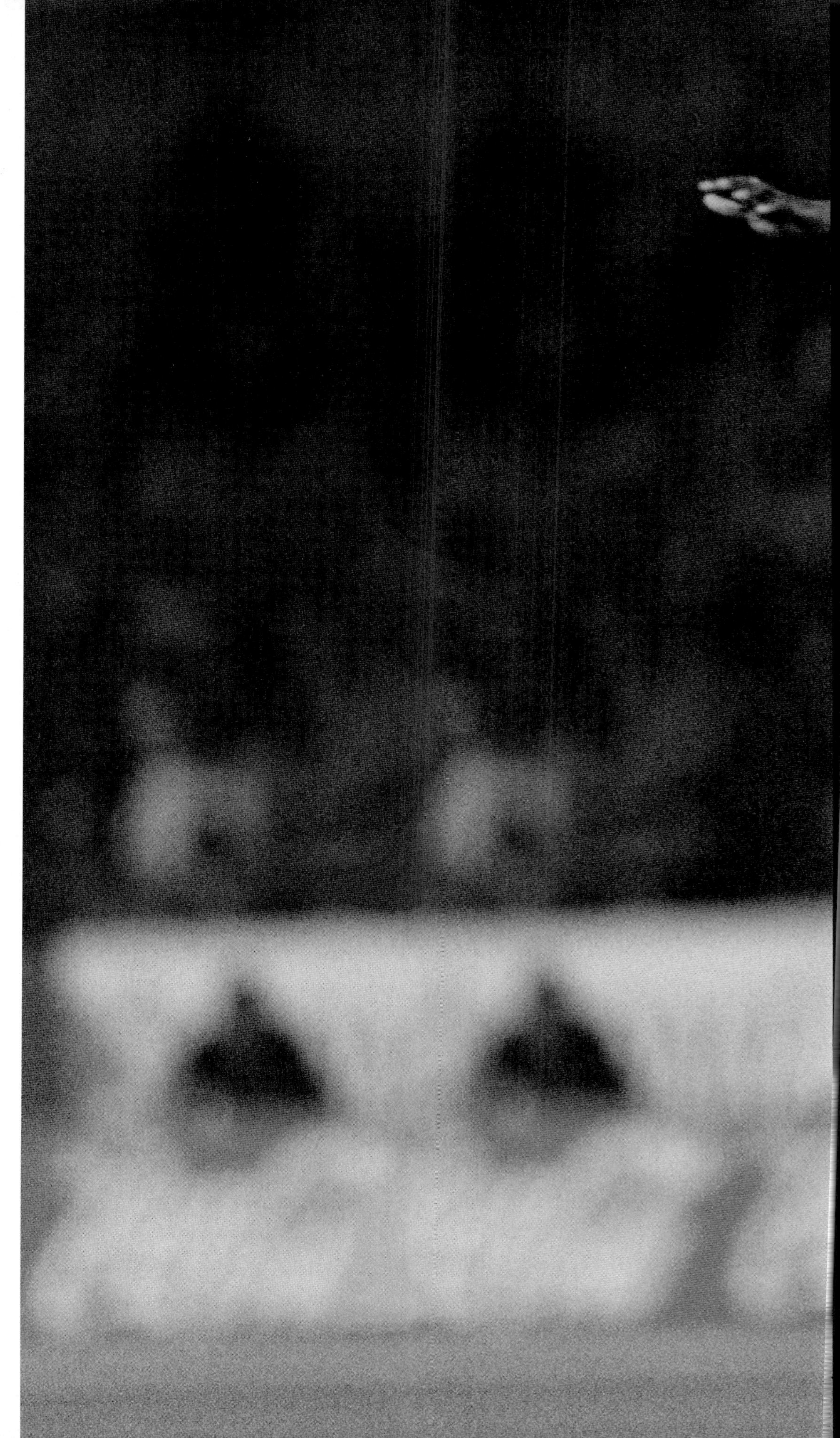

LA CORUÑA, Spain,
4 April 1996
A Coruña defender
puts his foot in it.

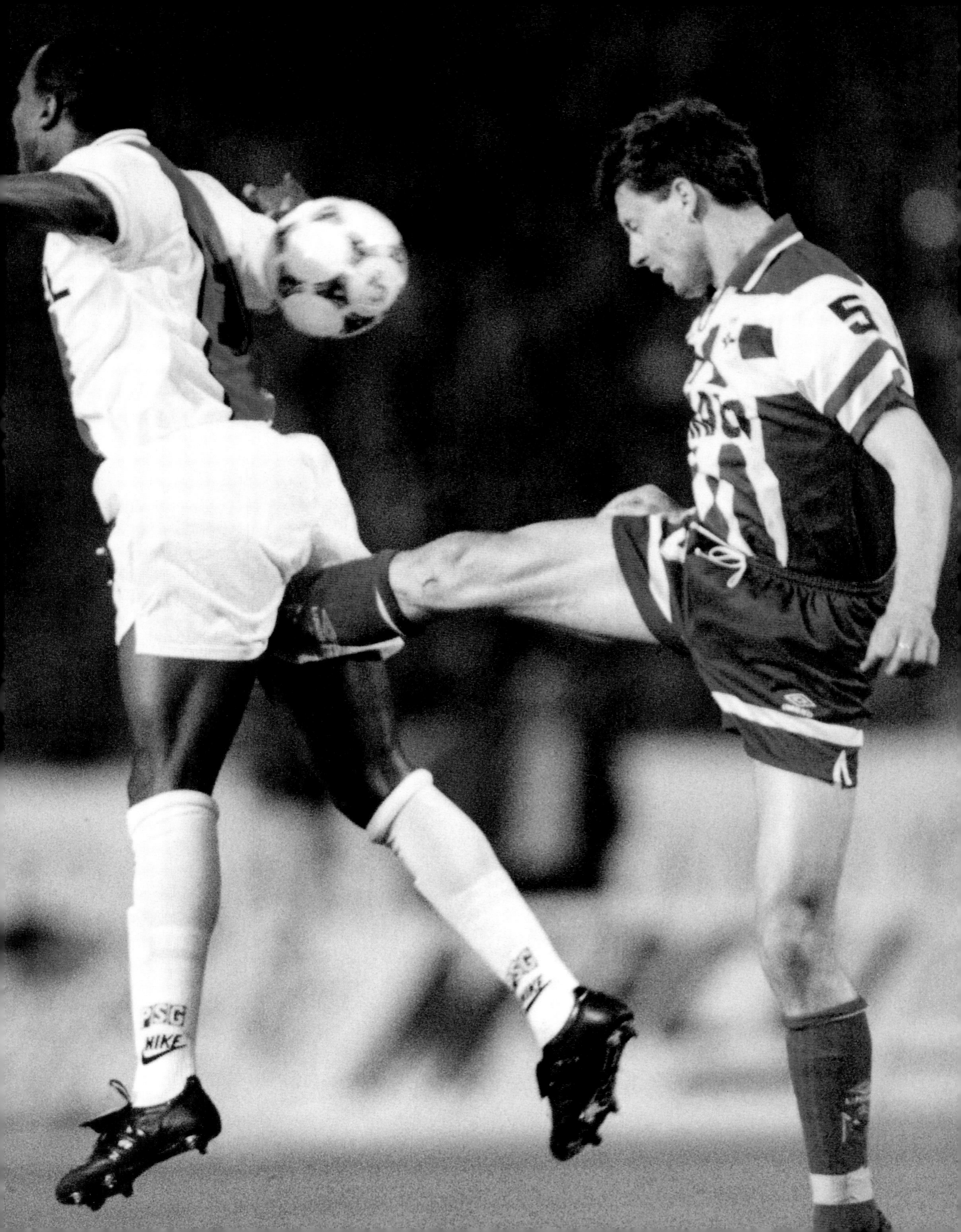

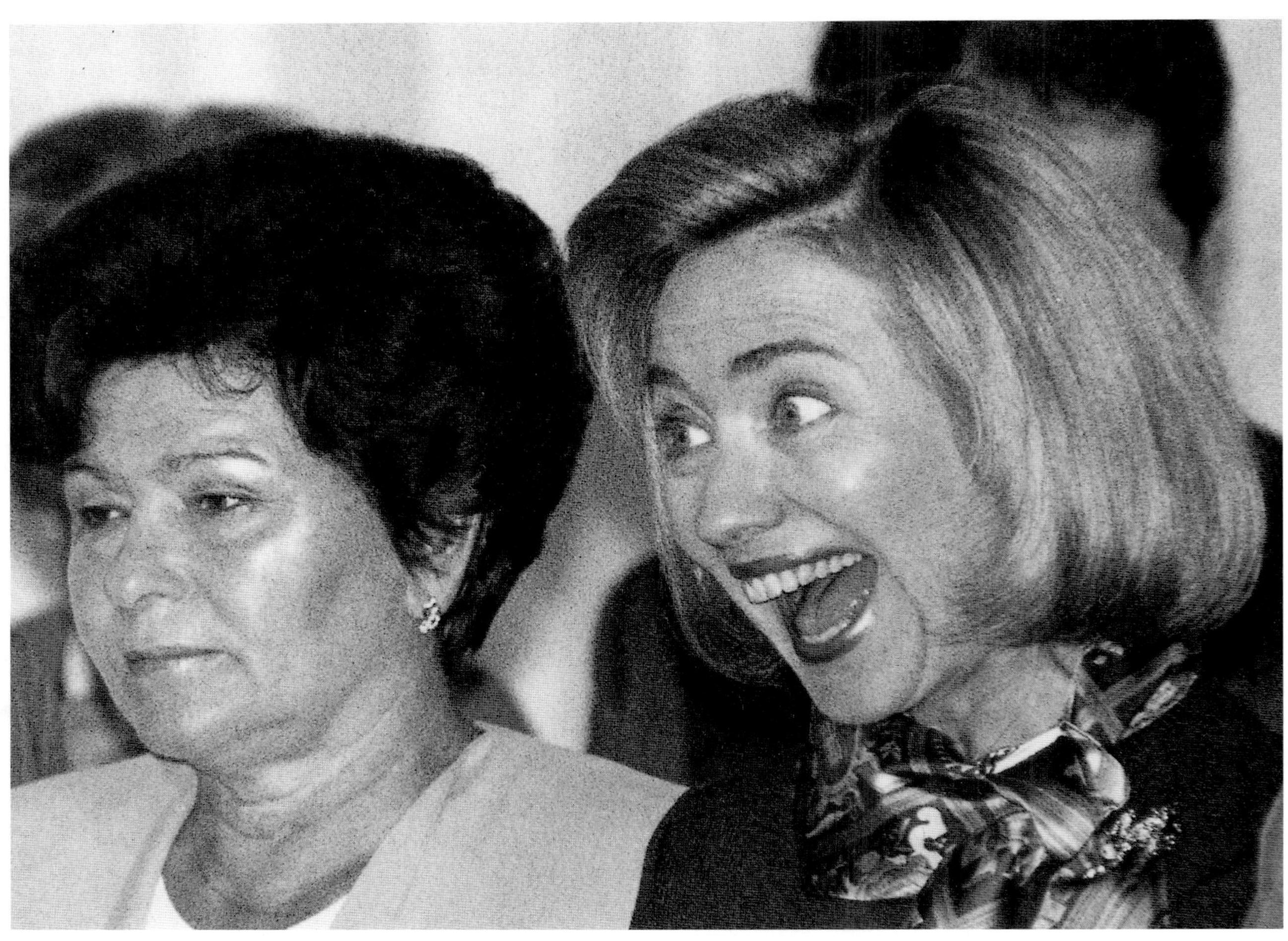

WASHINGTON, United States, 28 September 1994
**Official ceremony with Nania Yeltsin at the National Library of Congress
to celebrate the Russian Church in Alaska.**
More caviar!

WASHINGTON, United States, 12 April 1993
Easter celebrations at the White House
*After his success on the saxophone,
Bill Clinton opts for a simpler instrument
to make himself heard – a whistle.*

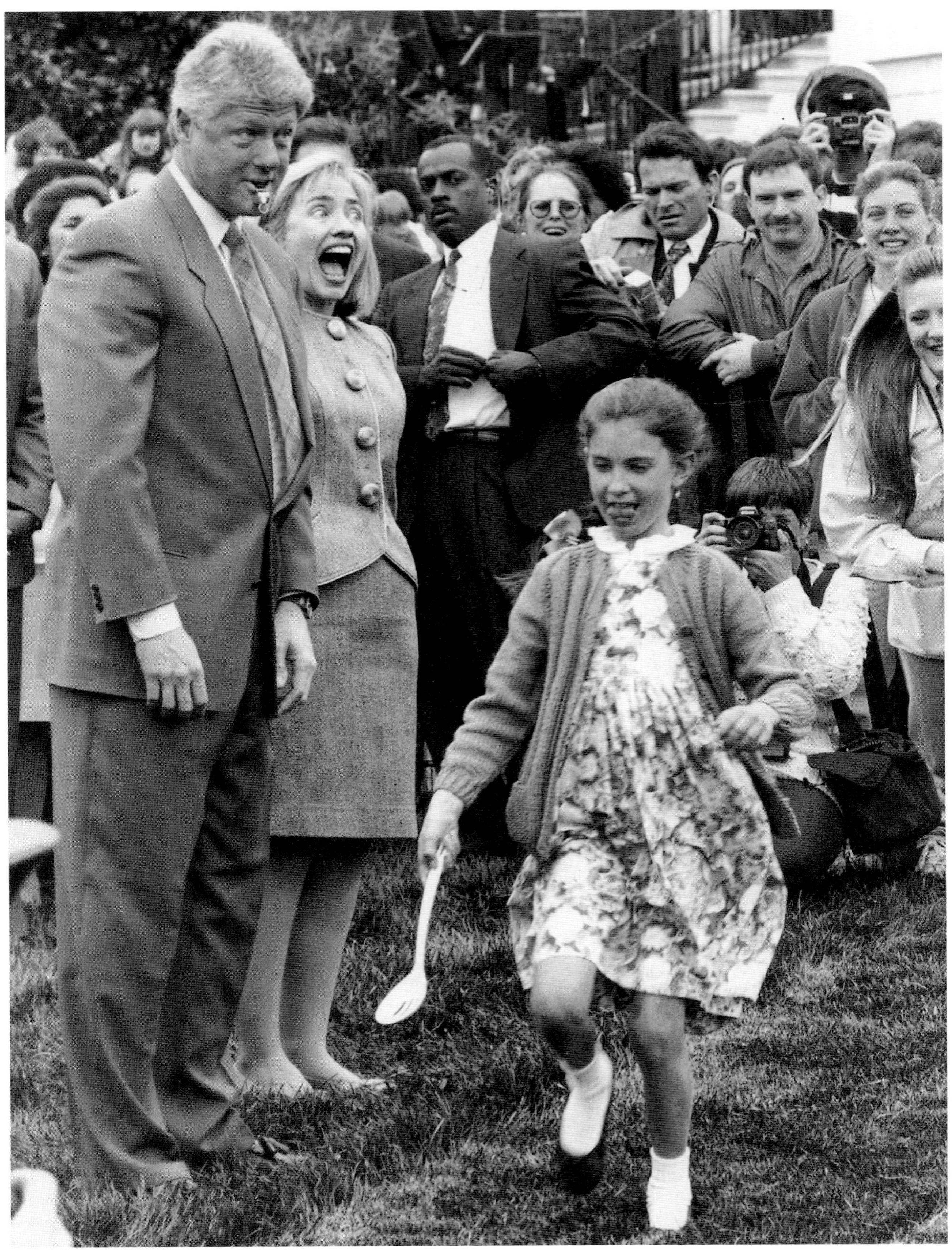

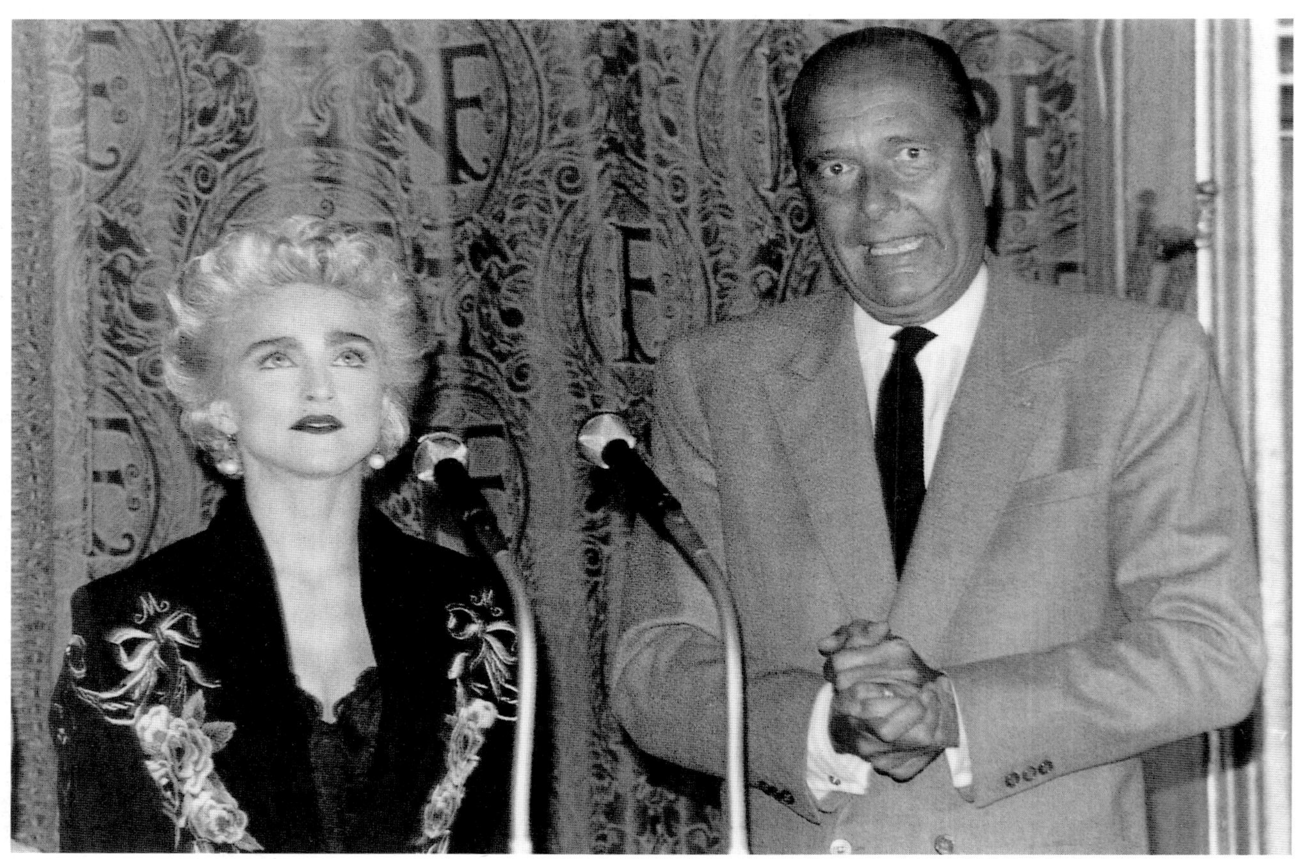

PARIS, France, 28 August 1987
Jacques Chirac, mayor of Paris, meets Madonna
I don't think we've been introduced.

PARIS, France, 5 December 1980
Politics is an obstacle course
*Jacques Chirac jumps a jammed barrier
at an exhibition of modern art at Auber station.*

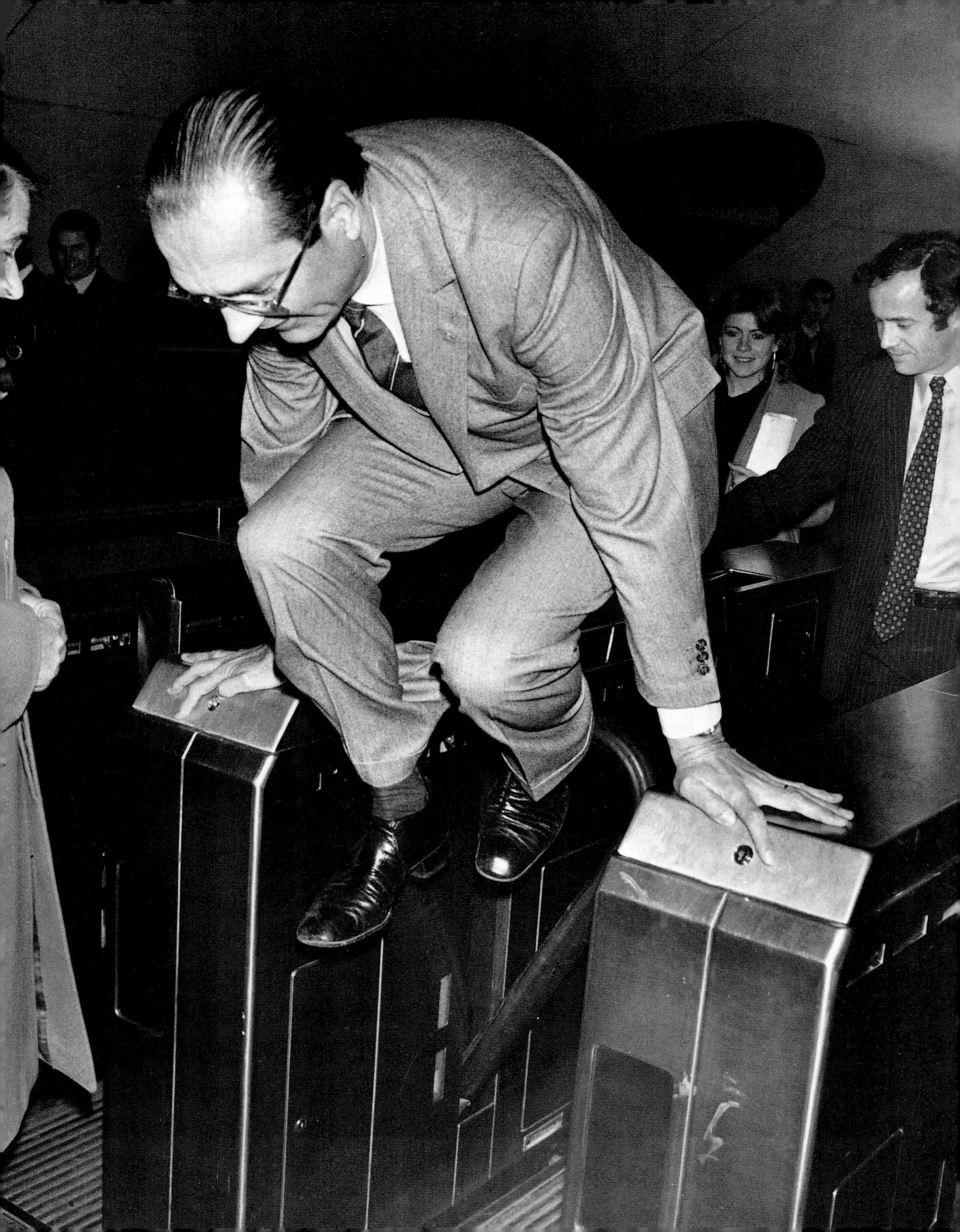

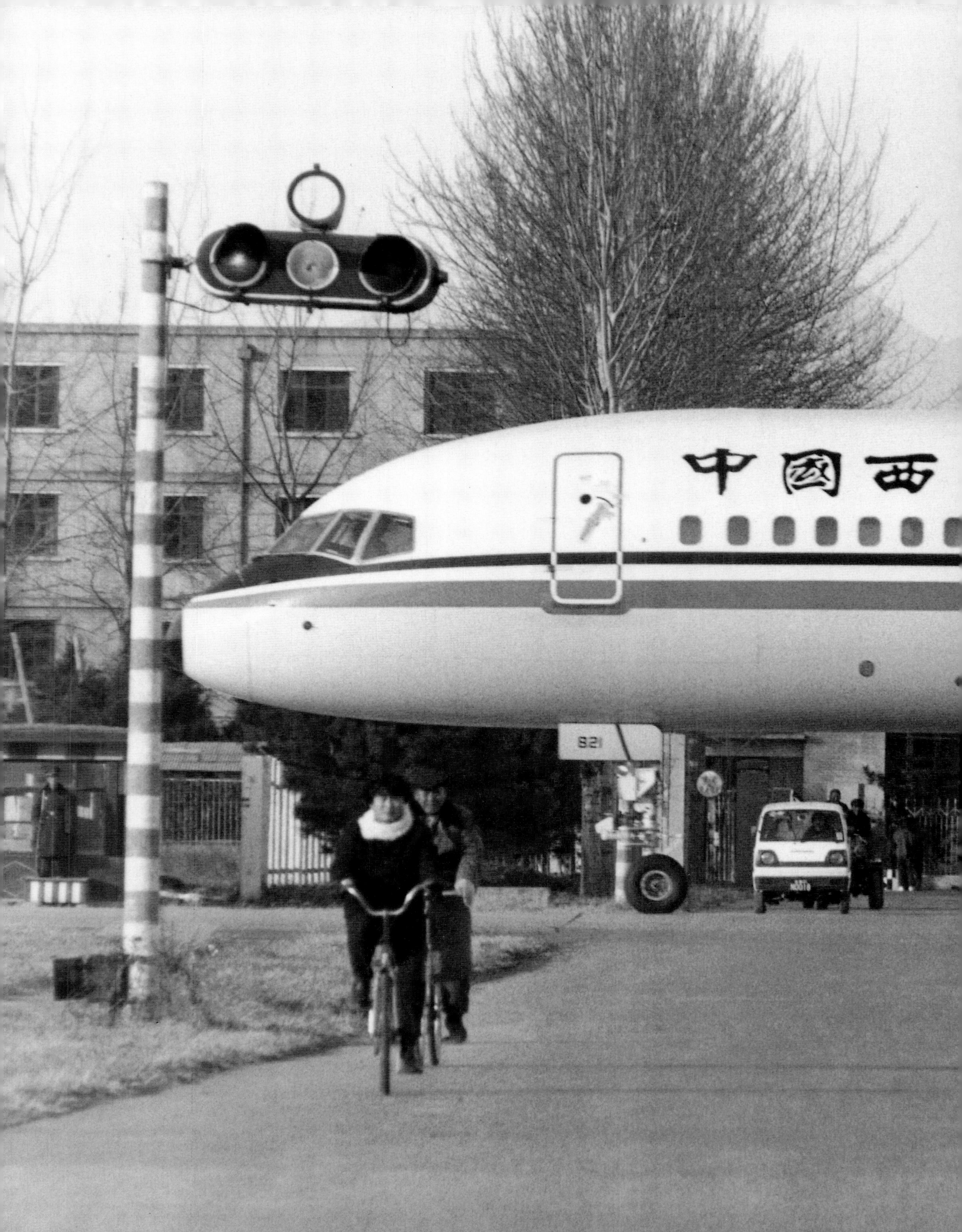

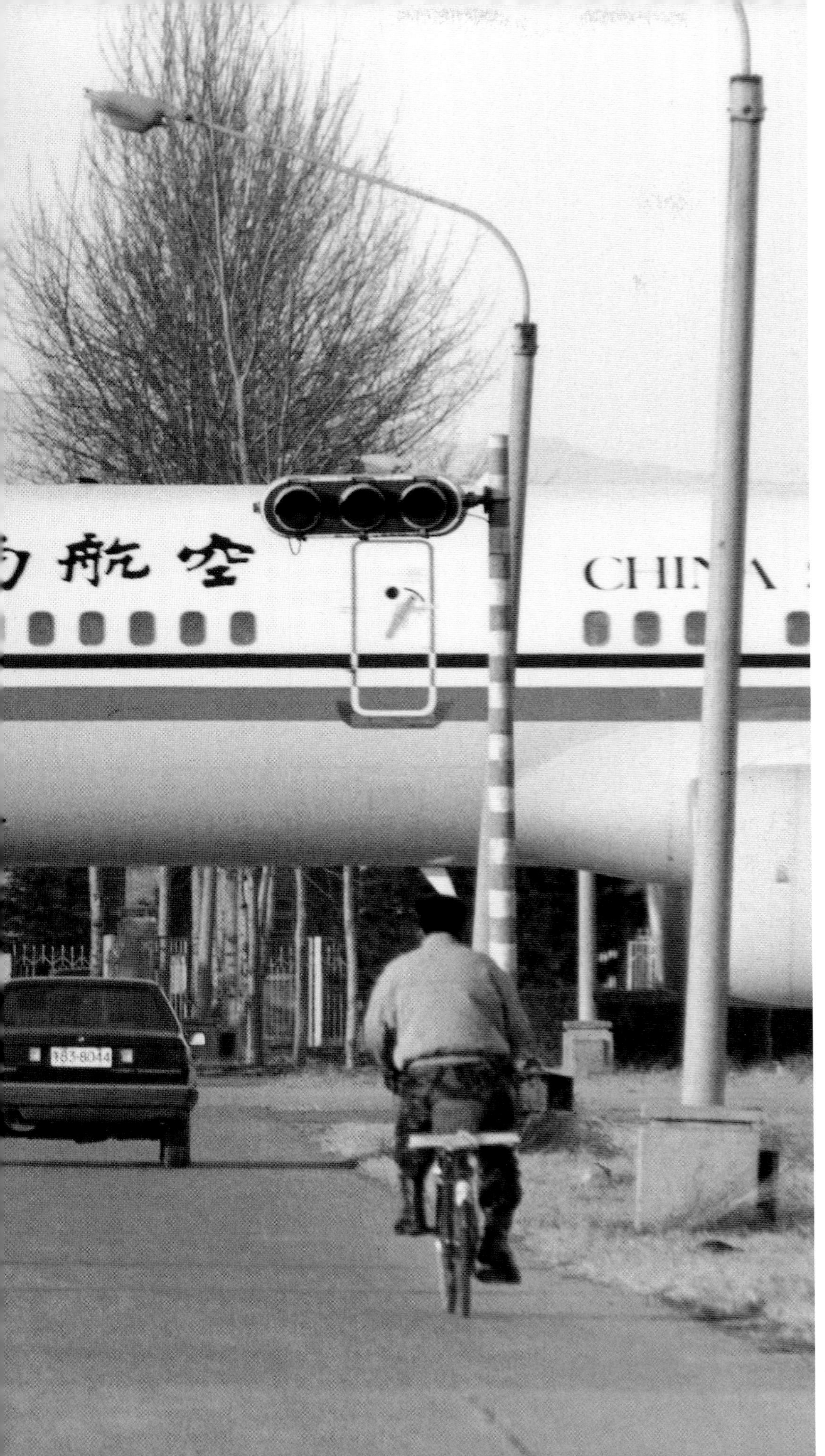

PEKING Airport, China,
1 December 1993
*Give way to vehicles
from right!*

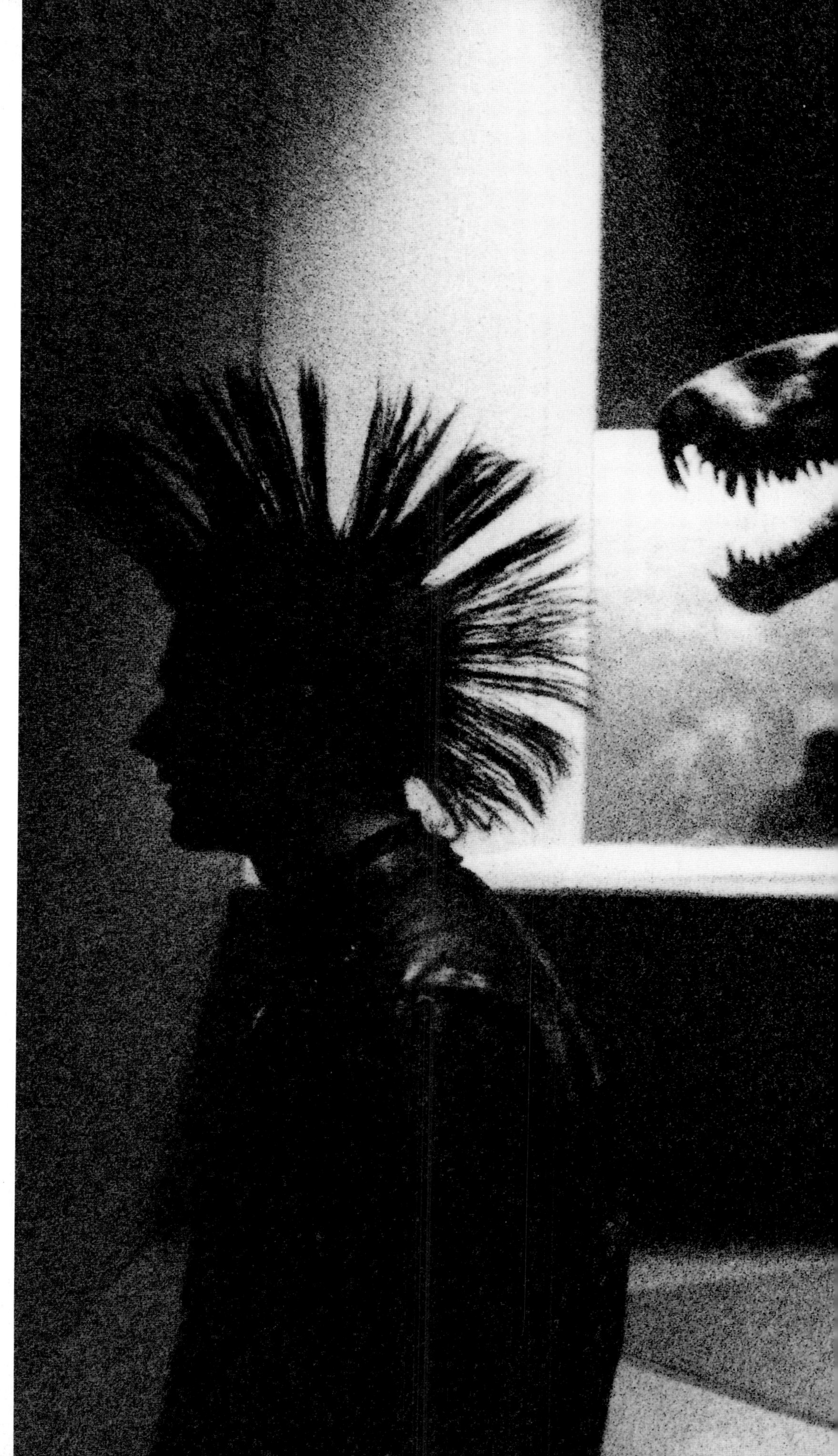

WASHINGTON,
United States,
8 January 1989
Exhibition
at the Museum
of Natural History
Hairstyles and attitudes.

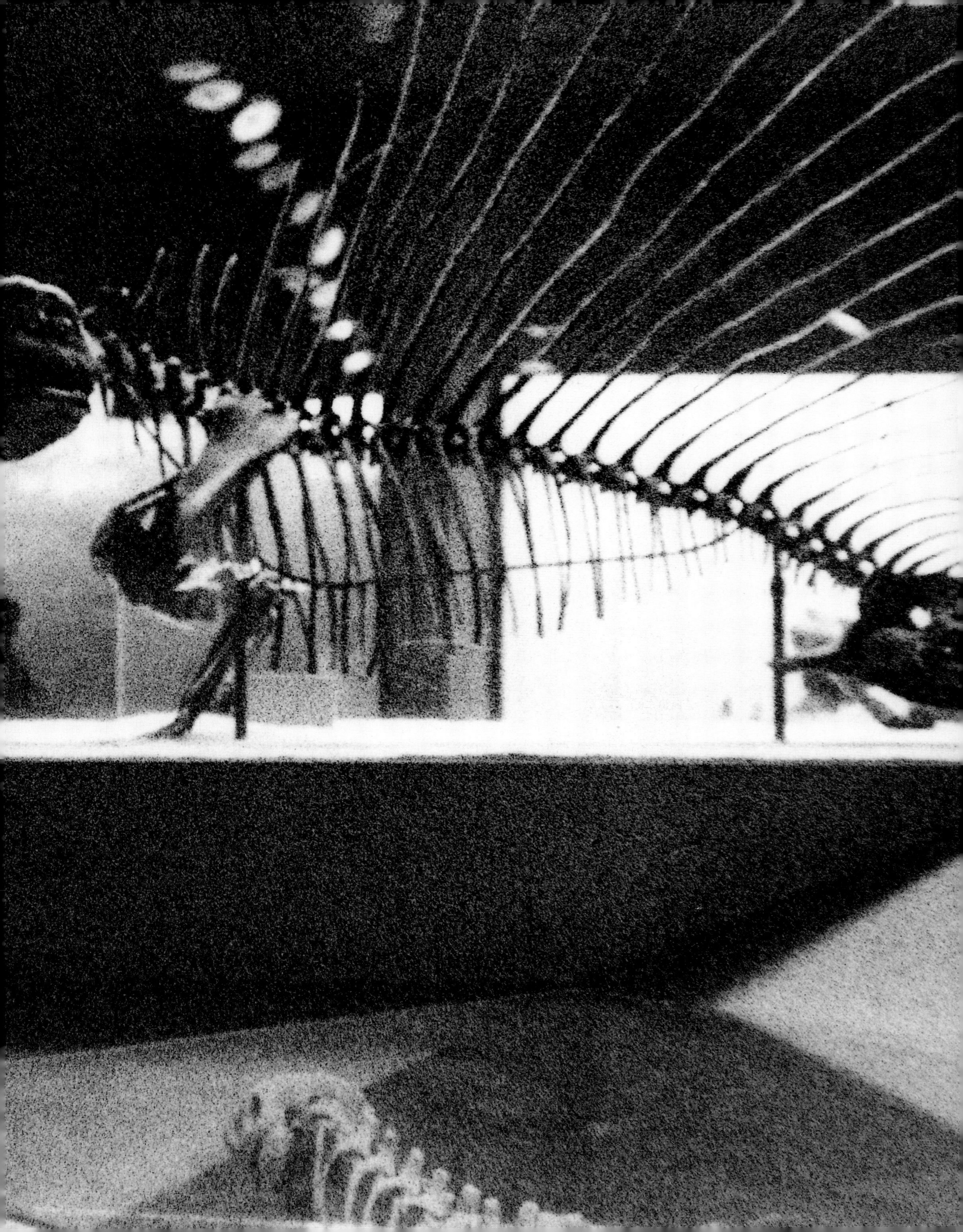

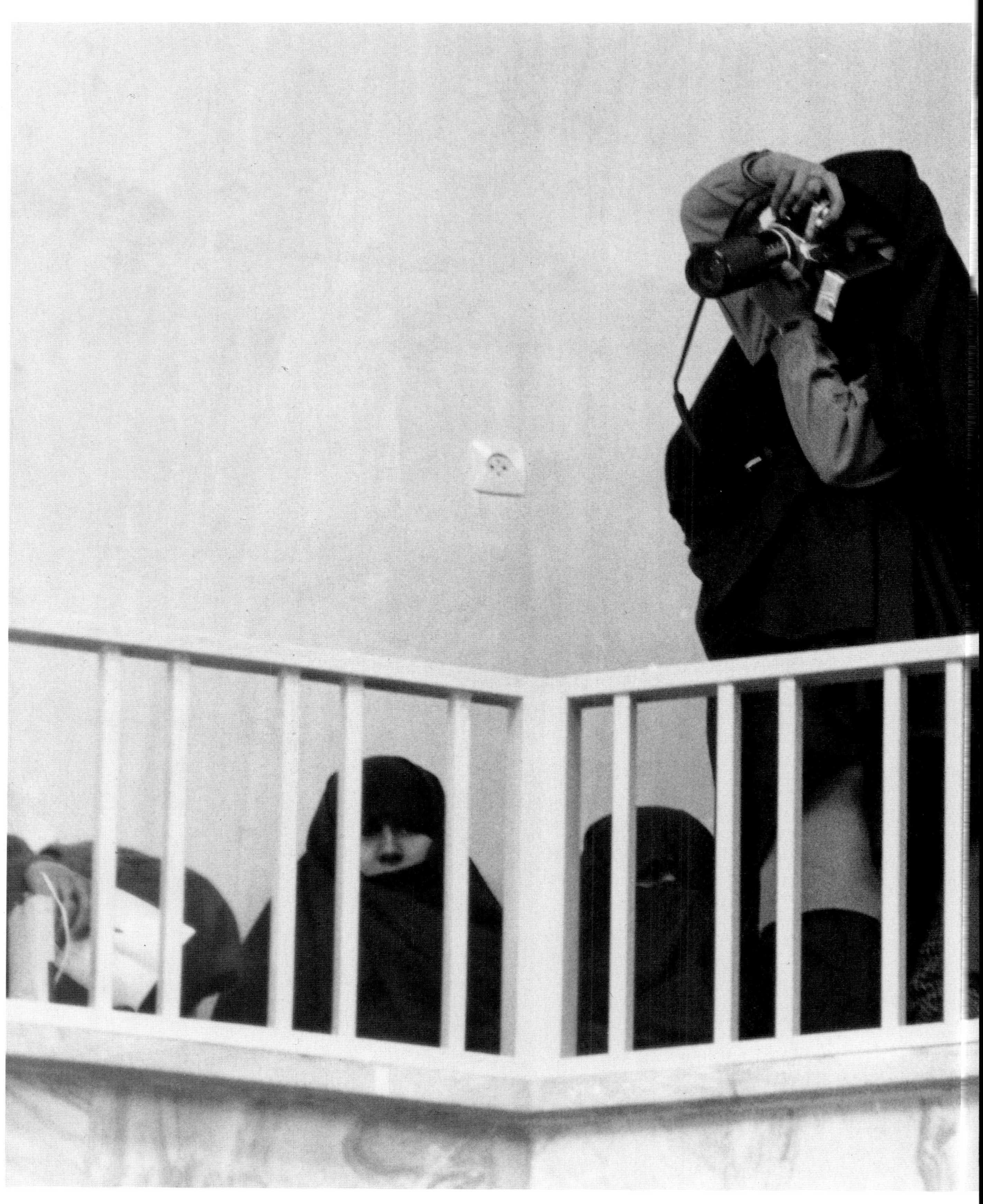

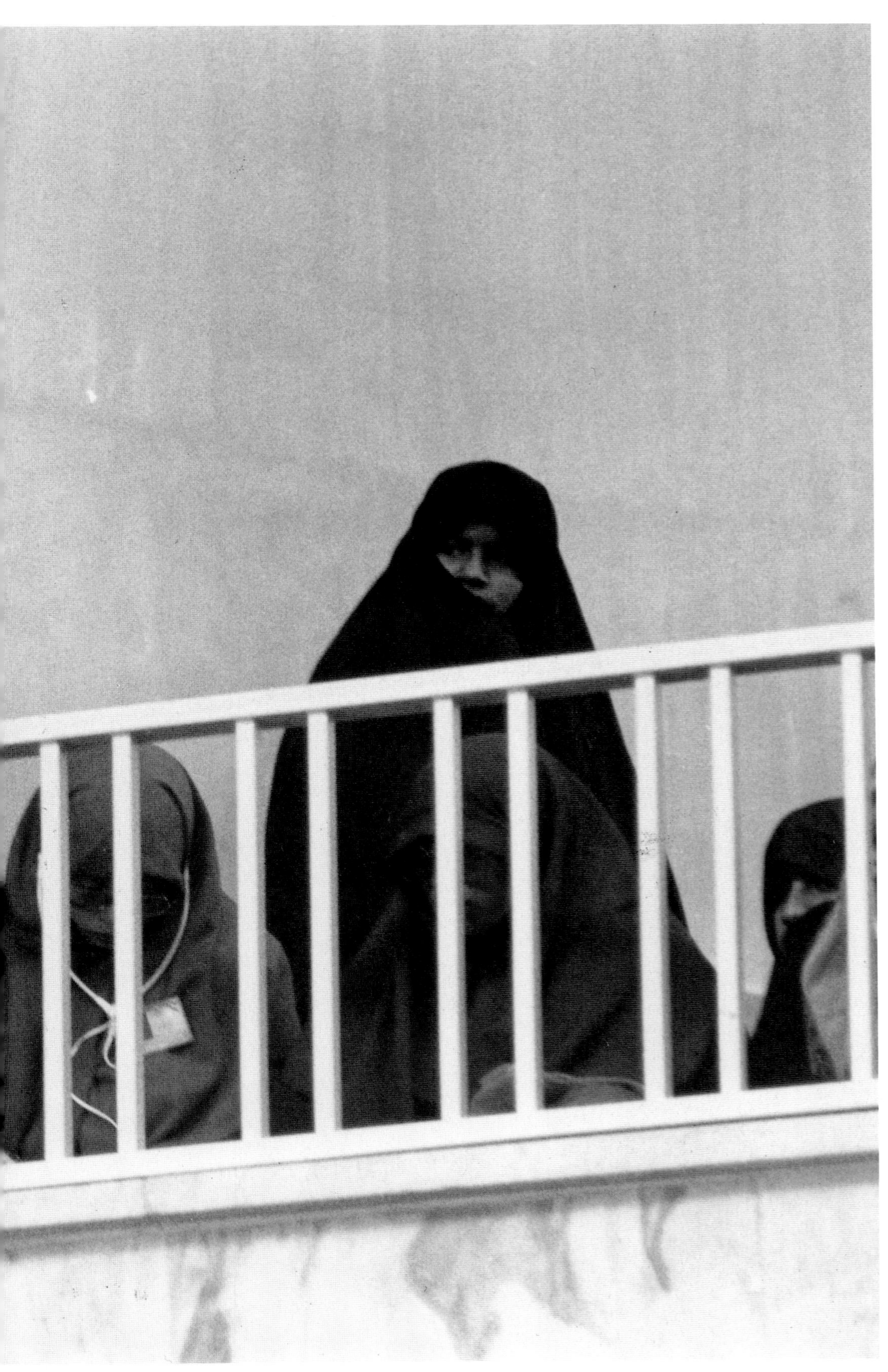

TEHRAN, Iran
**Women journalists
at a sitting of the
Chamber of Deputies**
*Luckily they were
not required to keep the
camera lens veiled as well.*

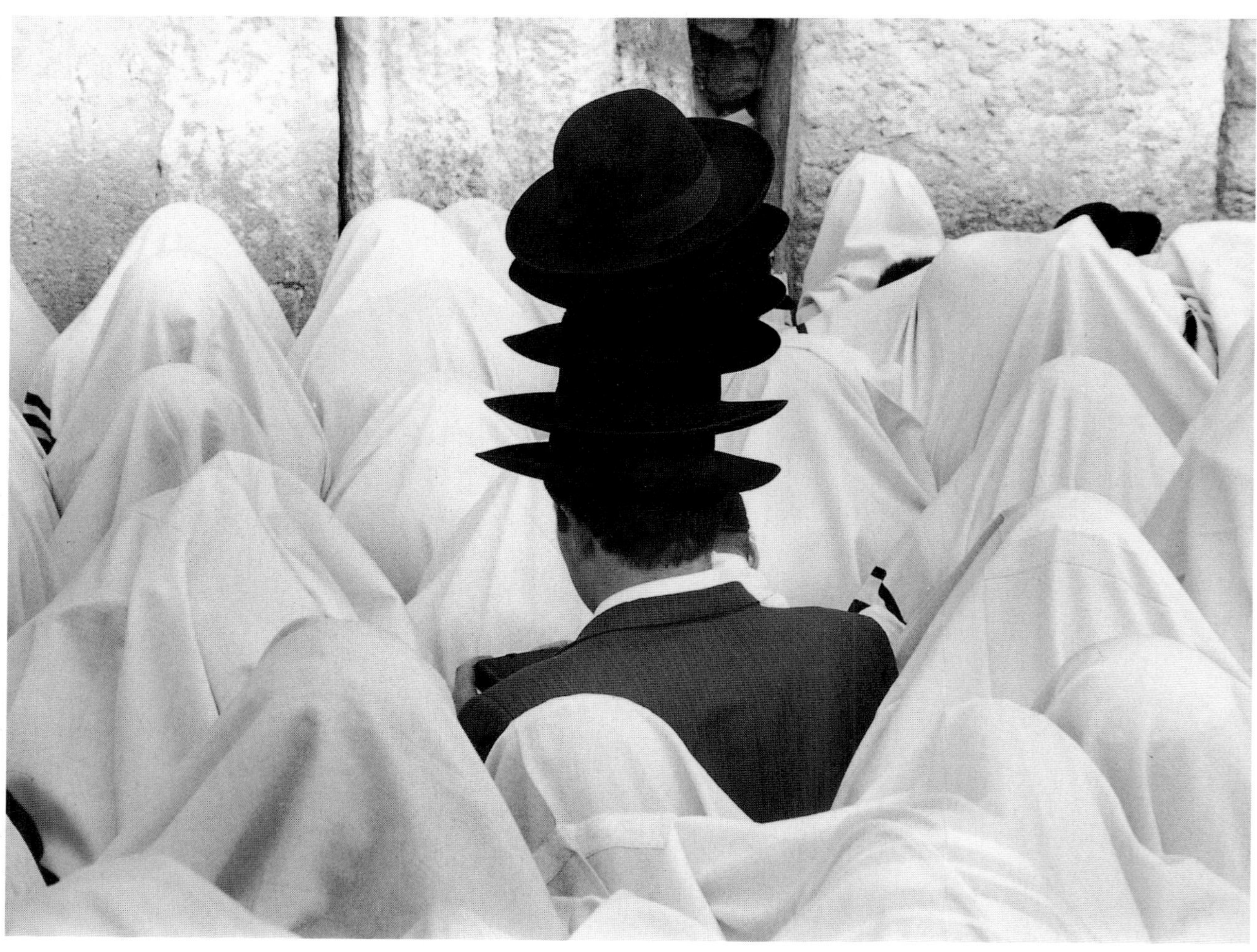

JERUSALEM, Israel, 8 April 1993
Jewish Easter
Keep you hat on!

MADISON SQUARE GARDEN,
New York, United States, 13 July 1992
Portofess – *Forgiveness on wheels.*

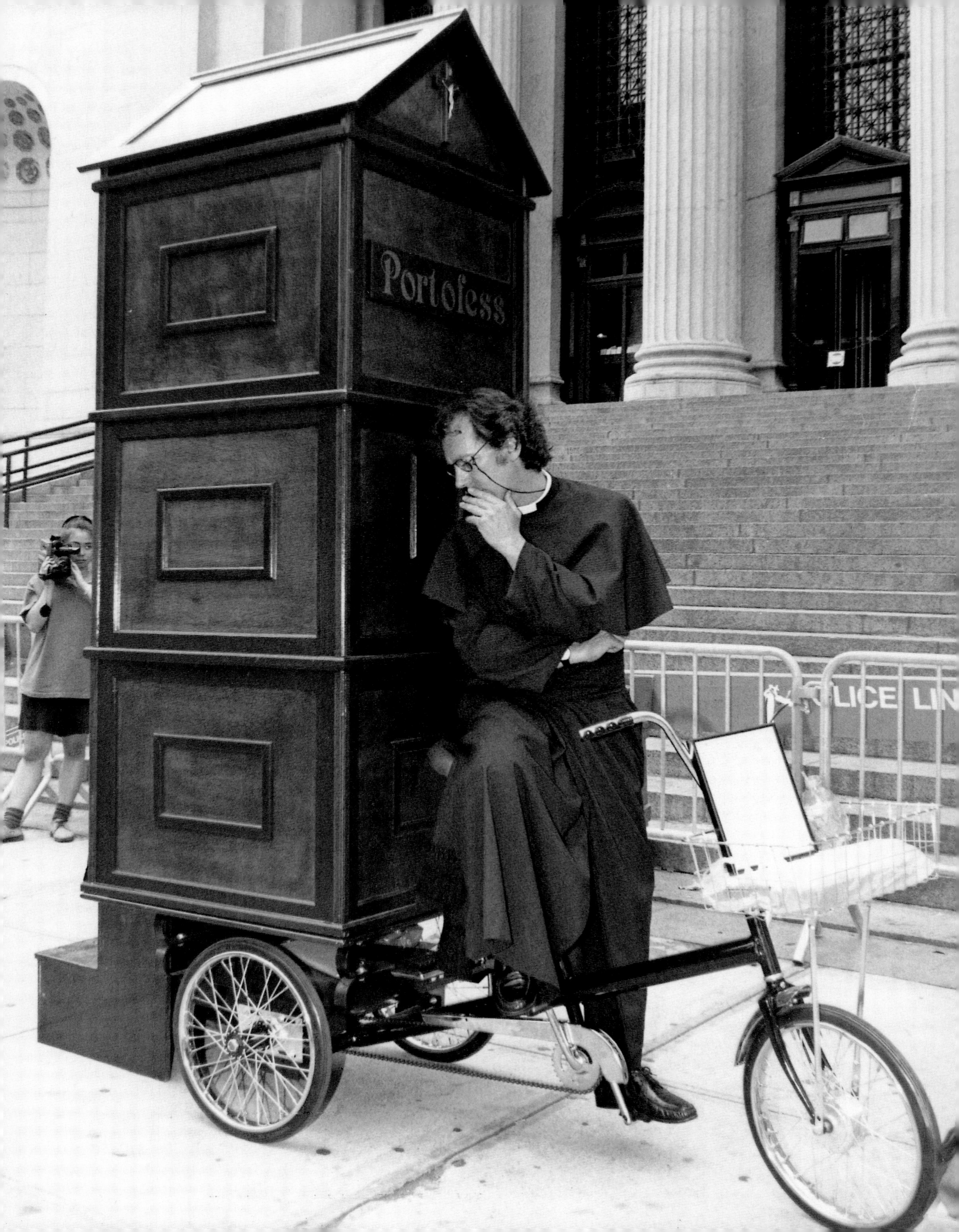

Portofess

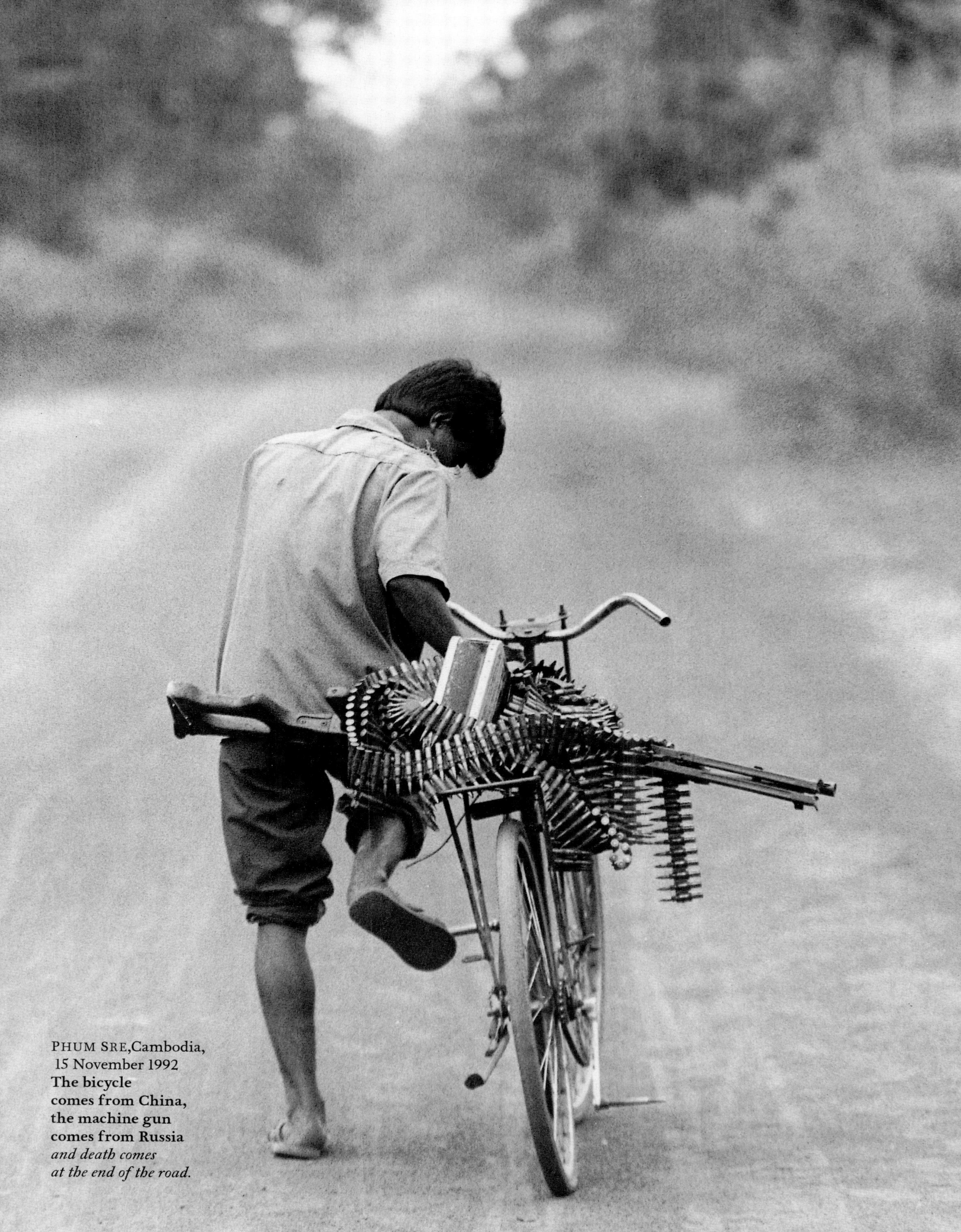

PHUM SRE, Cambodia,
15 November 1992
**The bicycle
comes from China,
the machine gun
comes from Russia**
*and death comes
at the end of the road.*

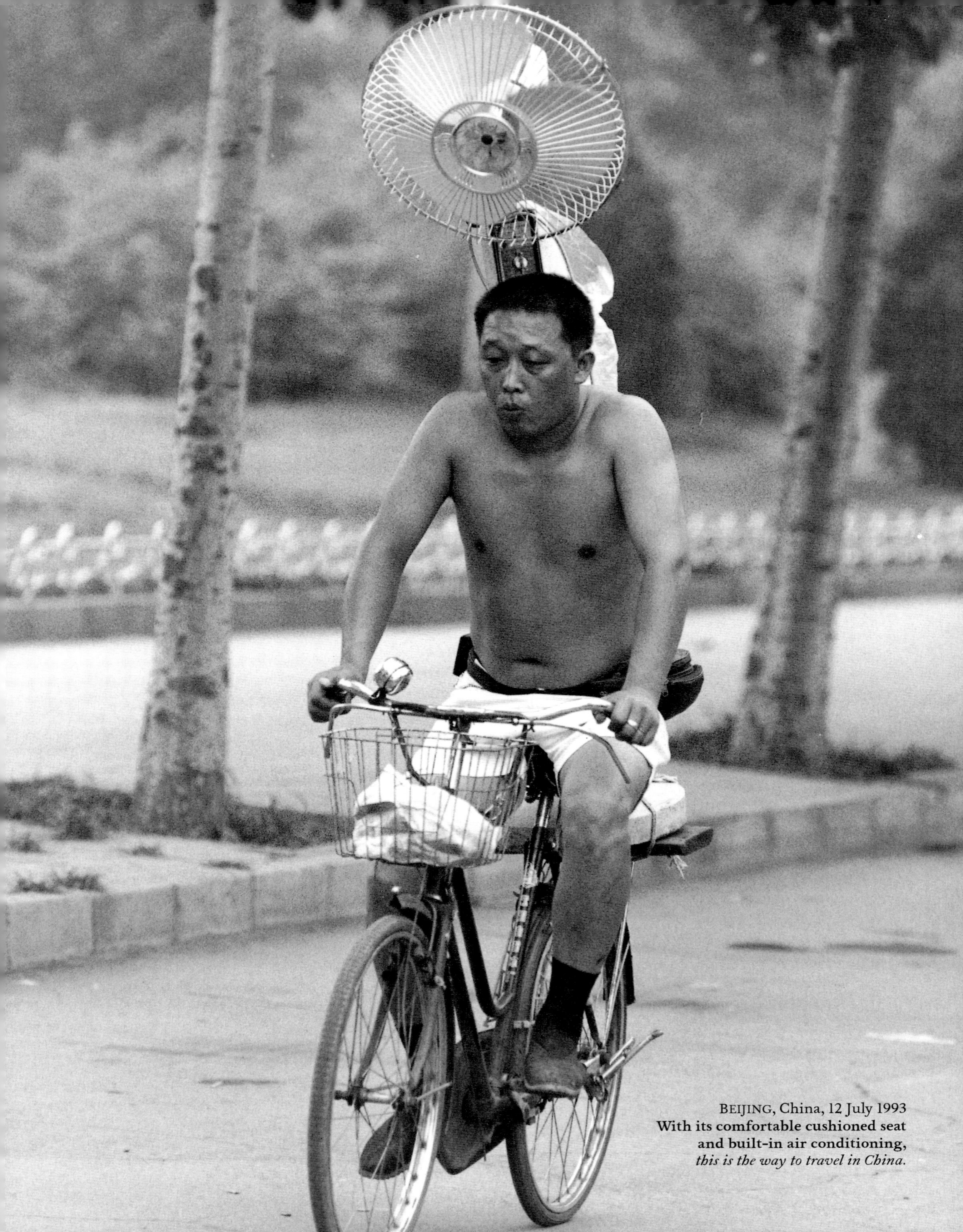

BEIJING, China, 12 July 1993
With its comfortable cushioned seat
and built-in air conditioning,
this is the way to travel in China.

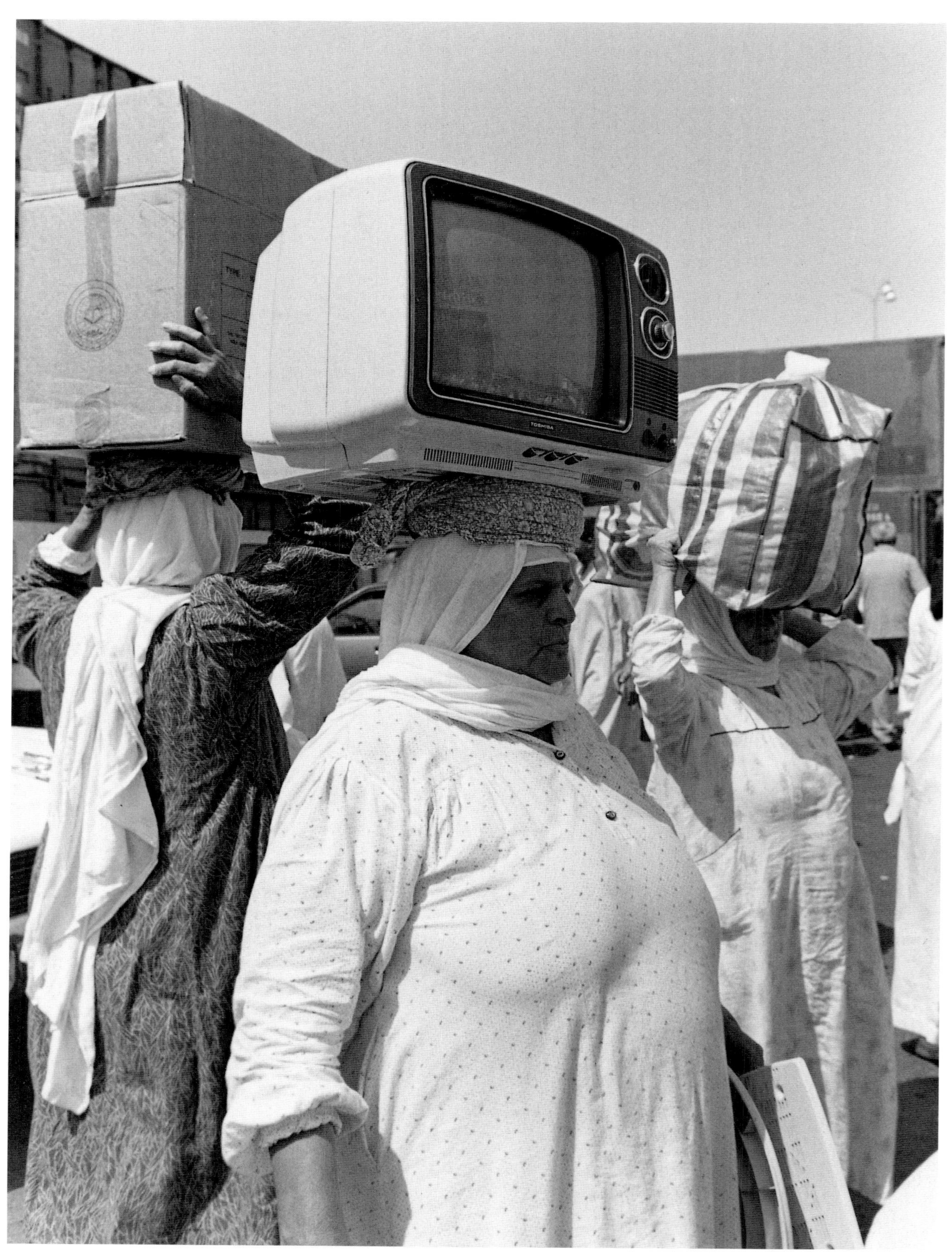

SUEZ, Egypt, 18 June 1992 **Return from a pilgrimage to Mecca.** *Look . . . no hands!*

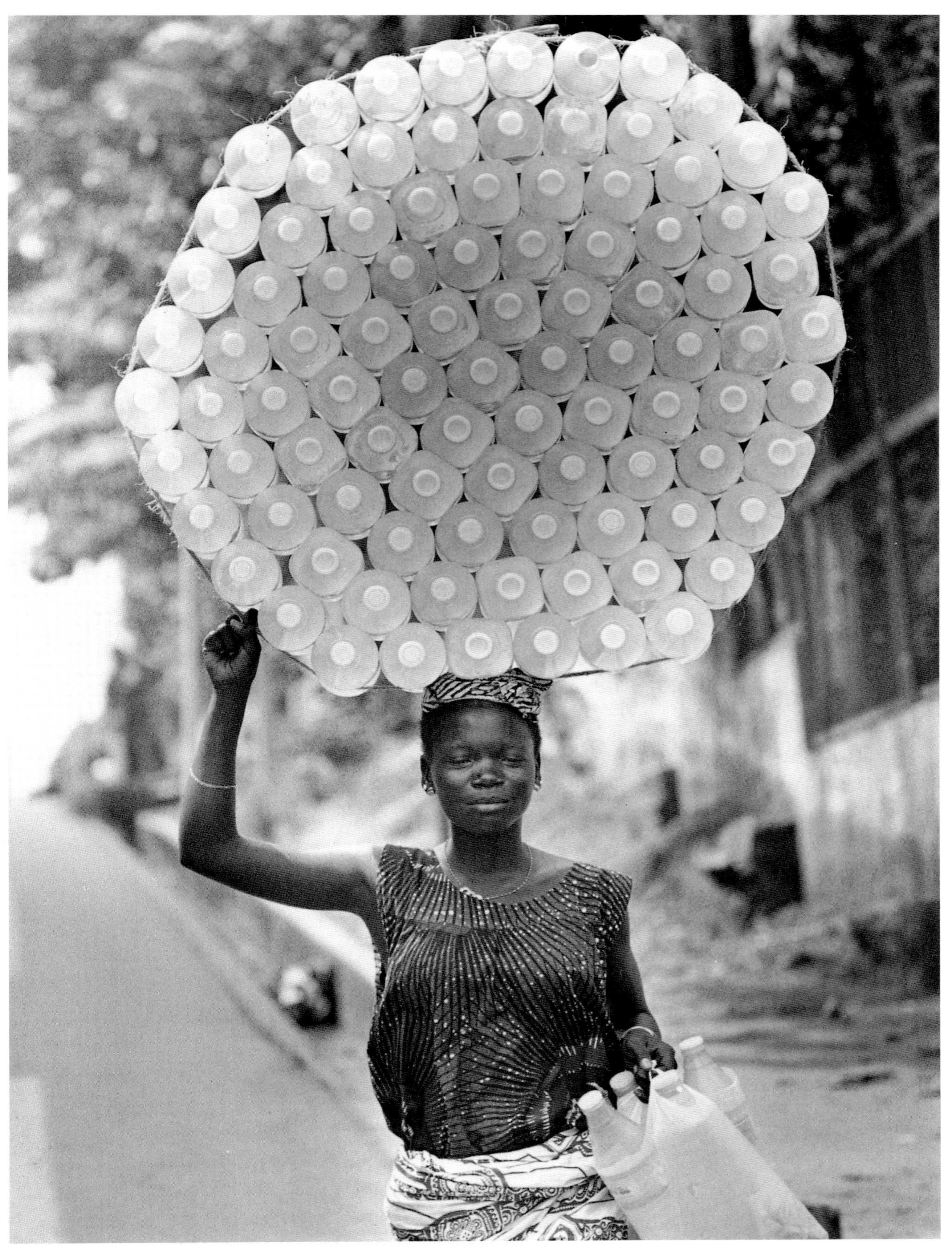

ABIDJAN, Ivory Coast, 6 March 1990. *Water on the brain.*

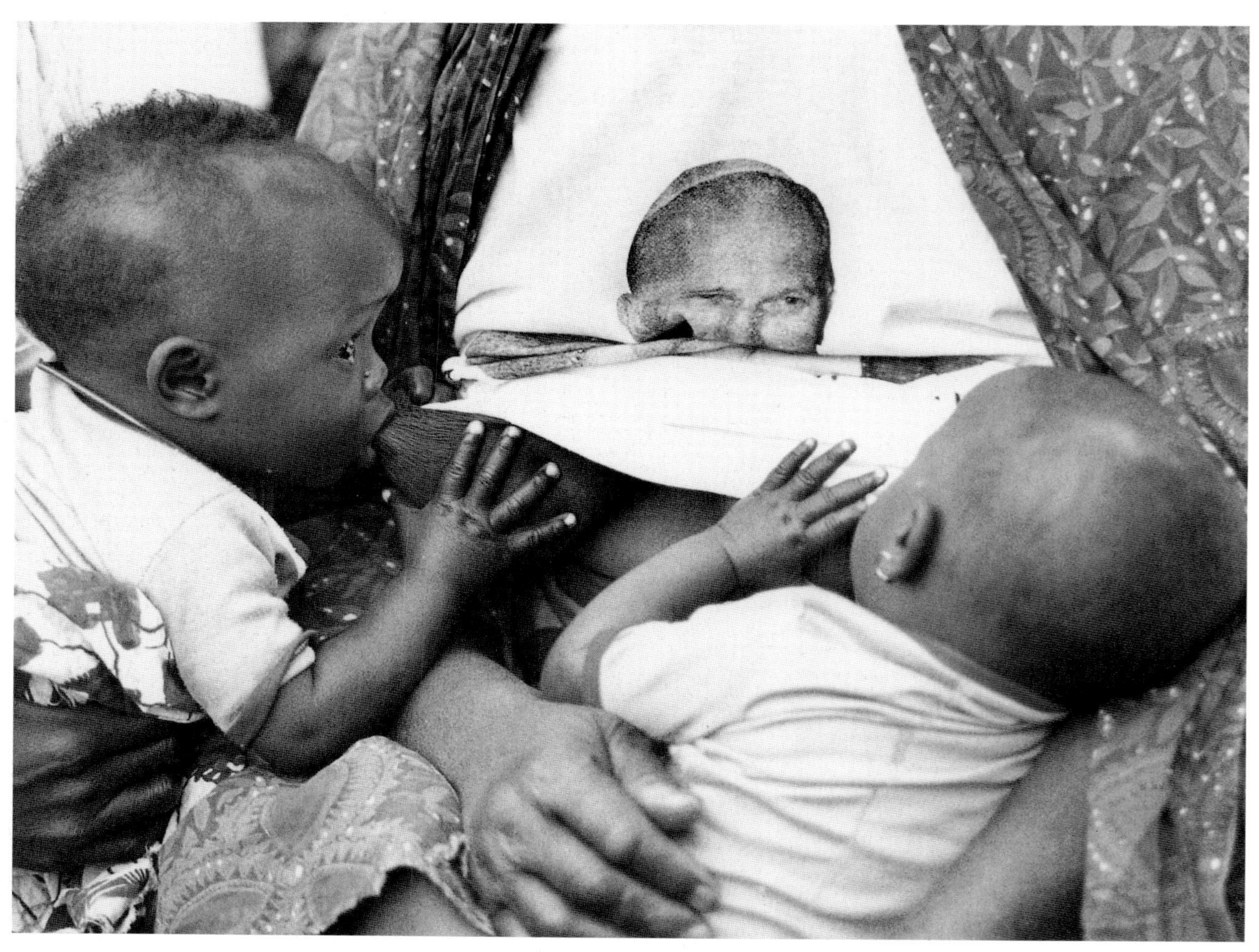

CUMURA, Guinea-Bissau, 28 January 1990
Papal visit to Africa
Like manna from heaven . . .

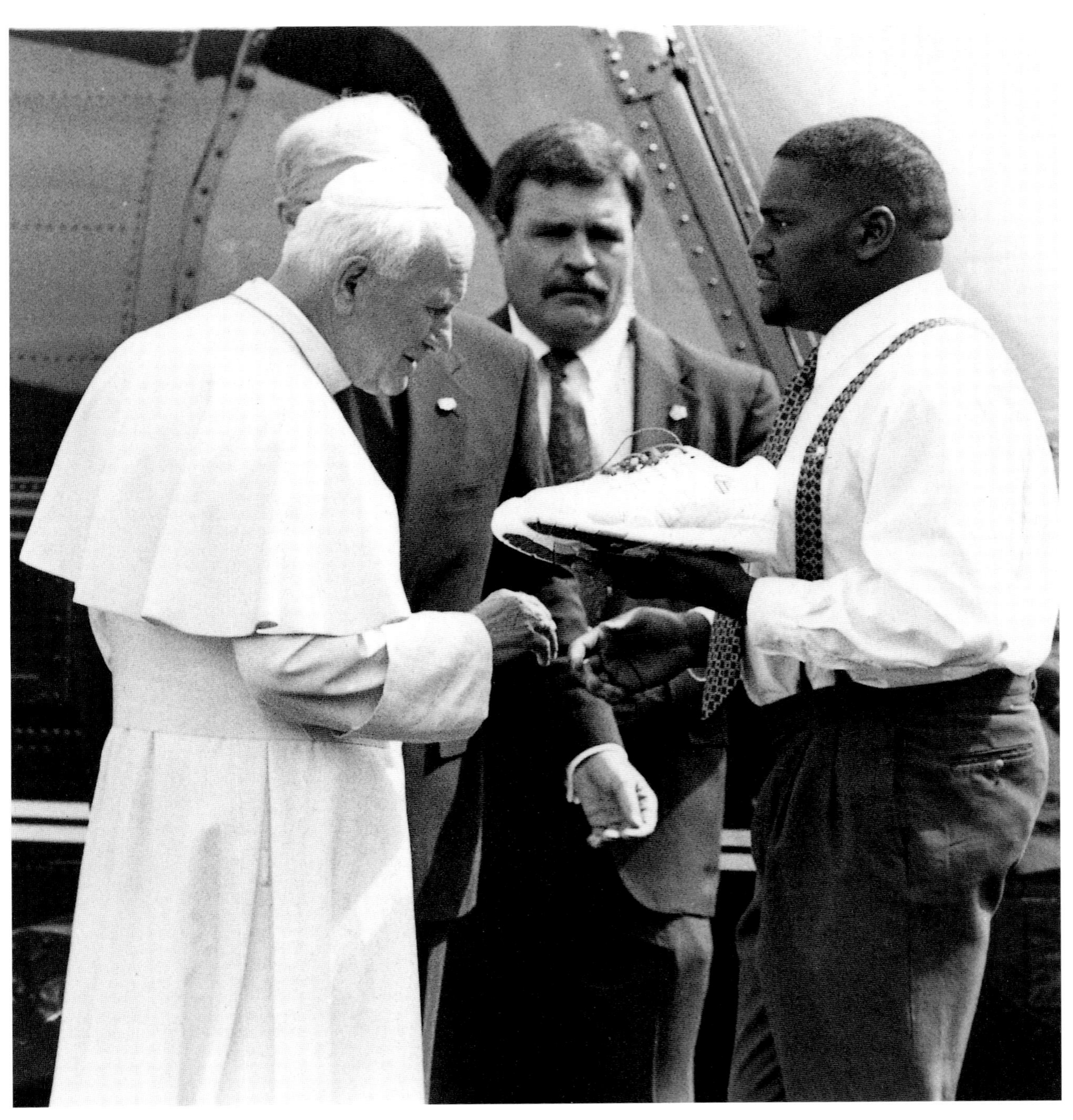

DENVER, United States, 13 August 1993
Eighth World Youth Day
Just Do It!

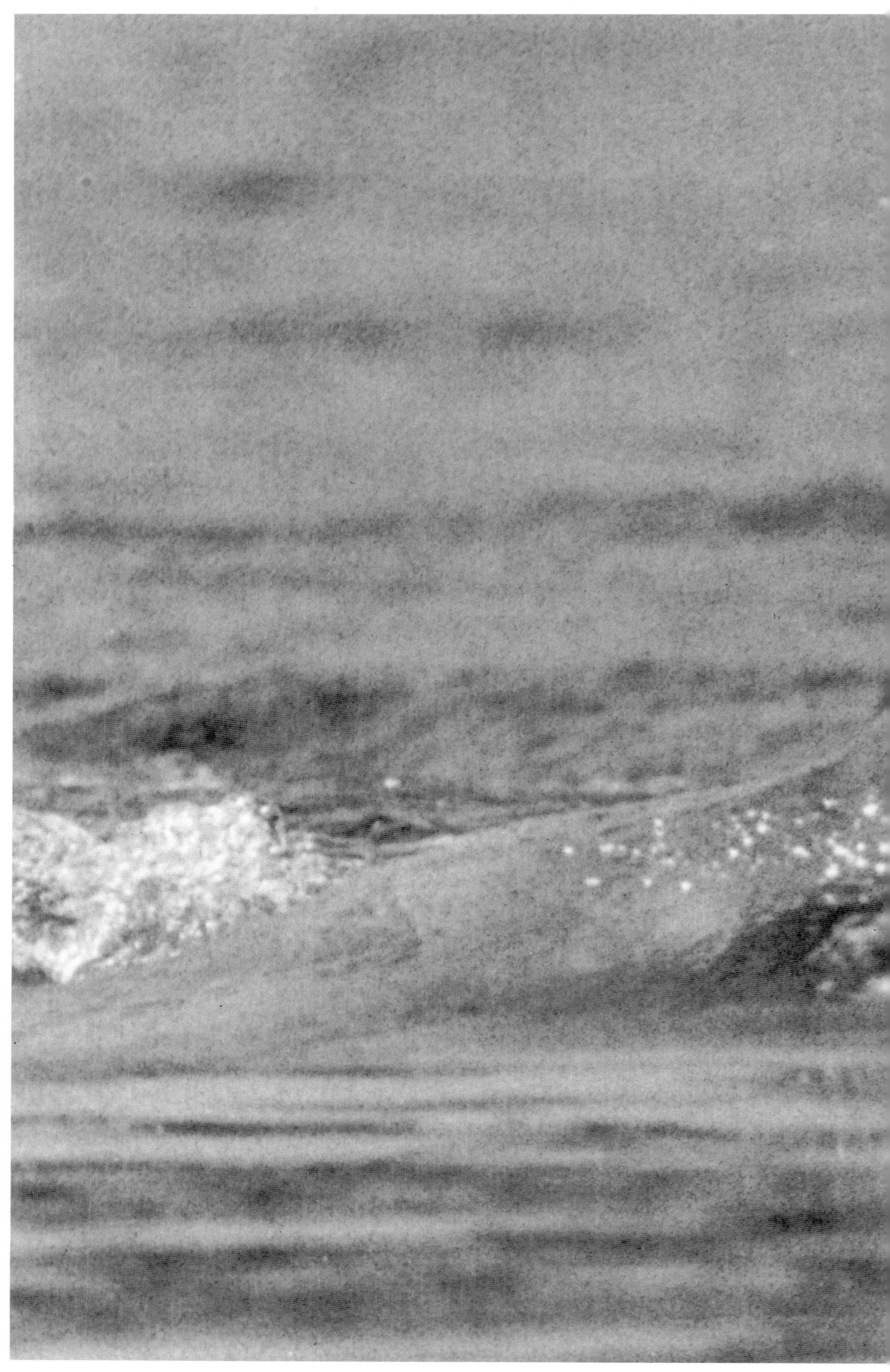

AUSTRIA,
25 August 1995
The Belgian
Frederik Deburghaeve
in the 200 m
freestyle race at the
European Swimming
Championships
*He went on to beat
the world record for 200 m
at the 1996 Olympic Games
in Atlanta.*

(Following double page)
TOULOUSE, France,
14 February 1996
Presentation
of the A320 Airbus
*While Prince Charles
contemplates the skies,
Jacques Chirac's
attention is attracted
by more earthly matters.*

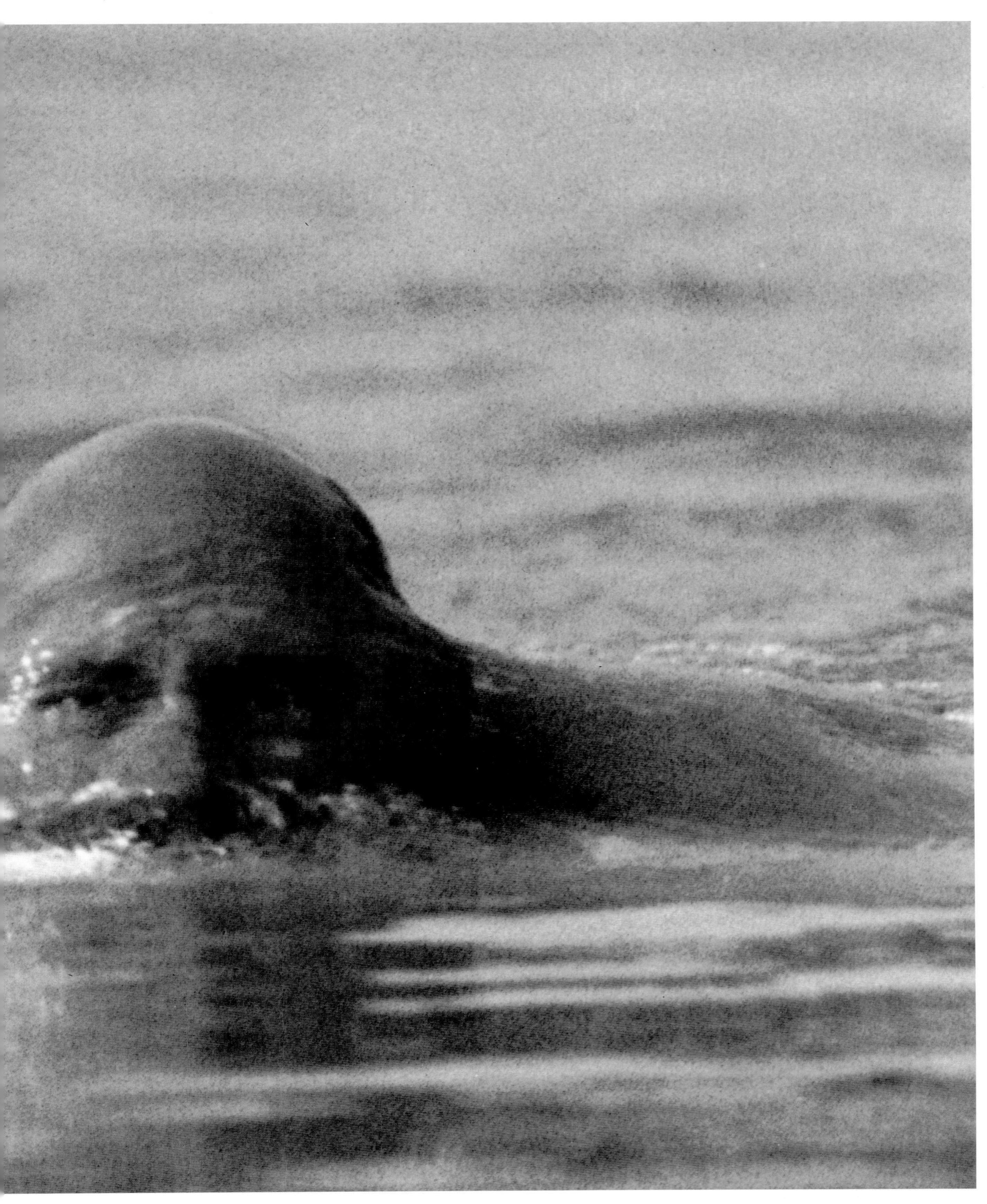

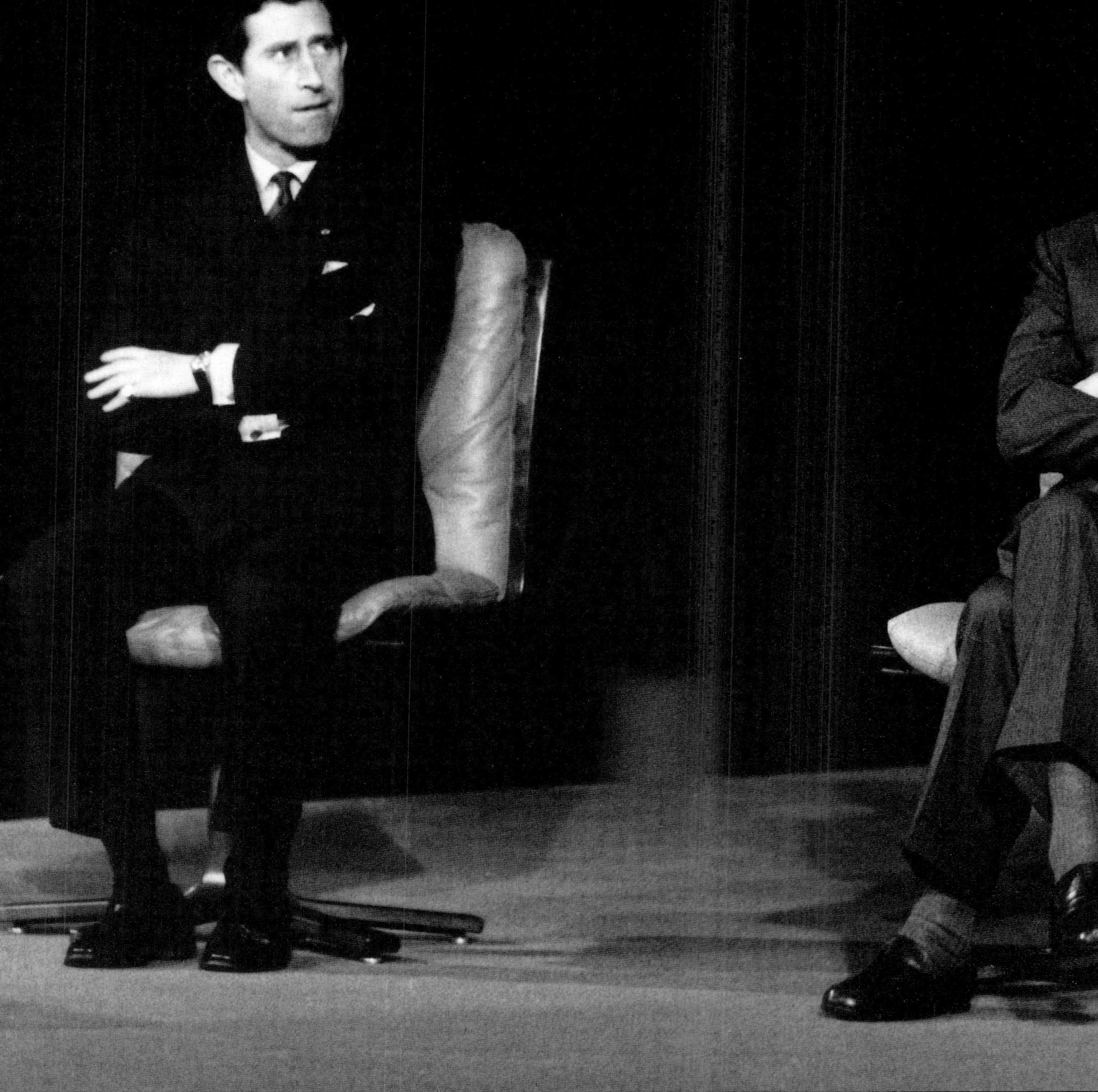

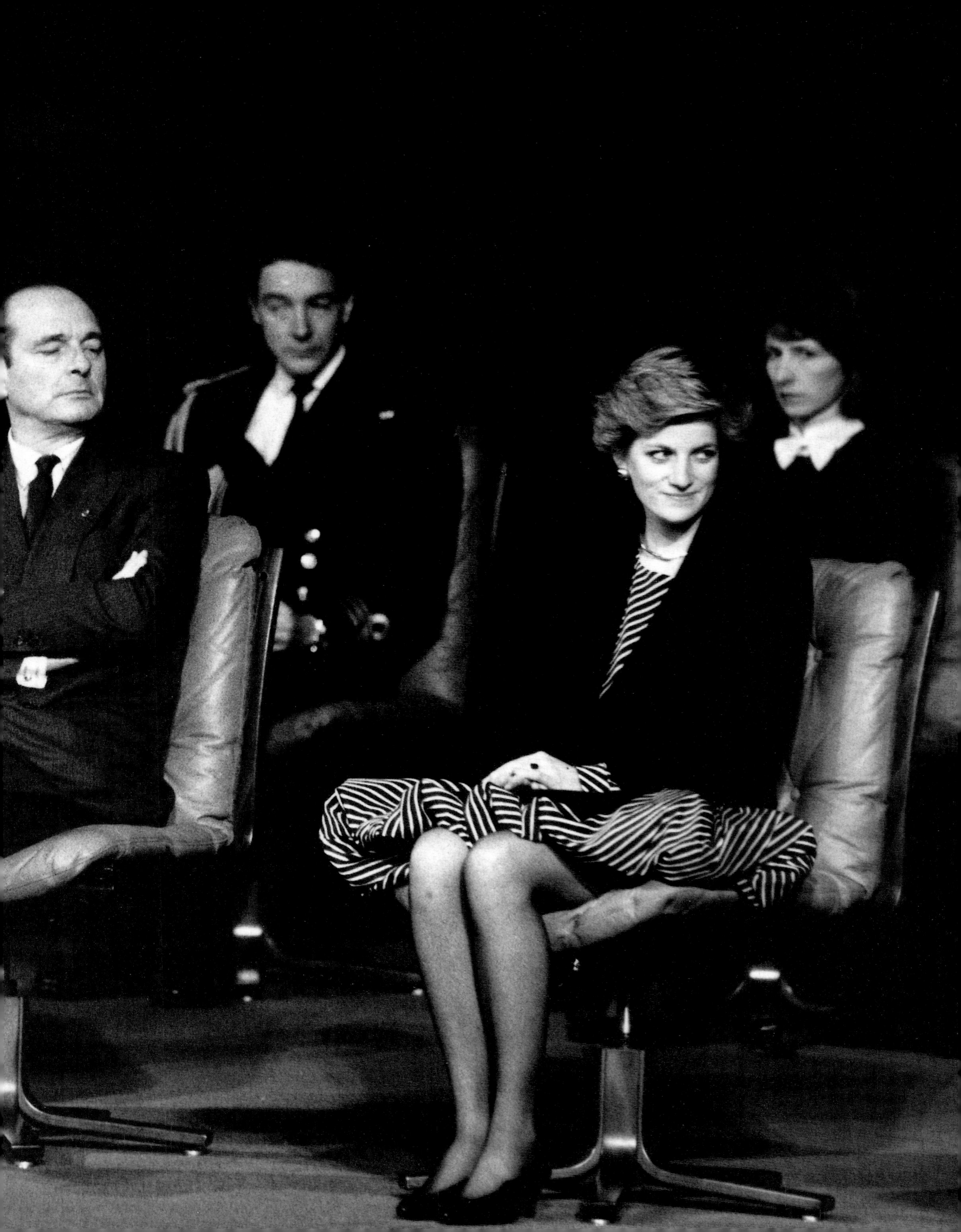

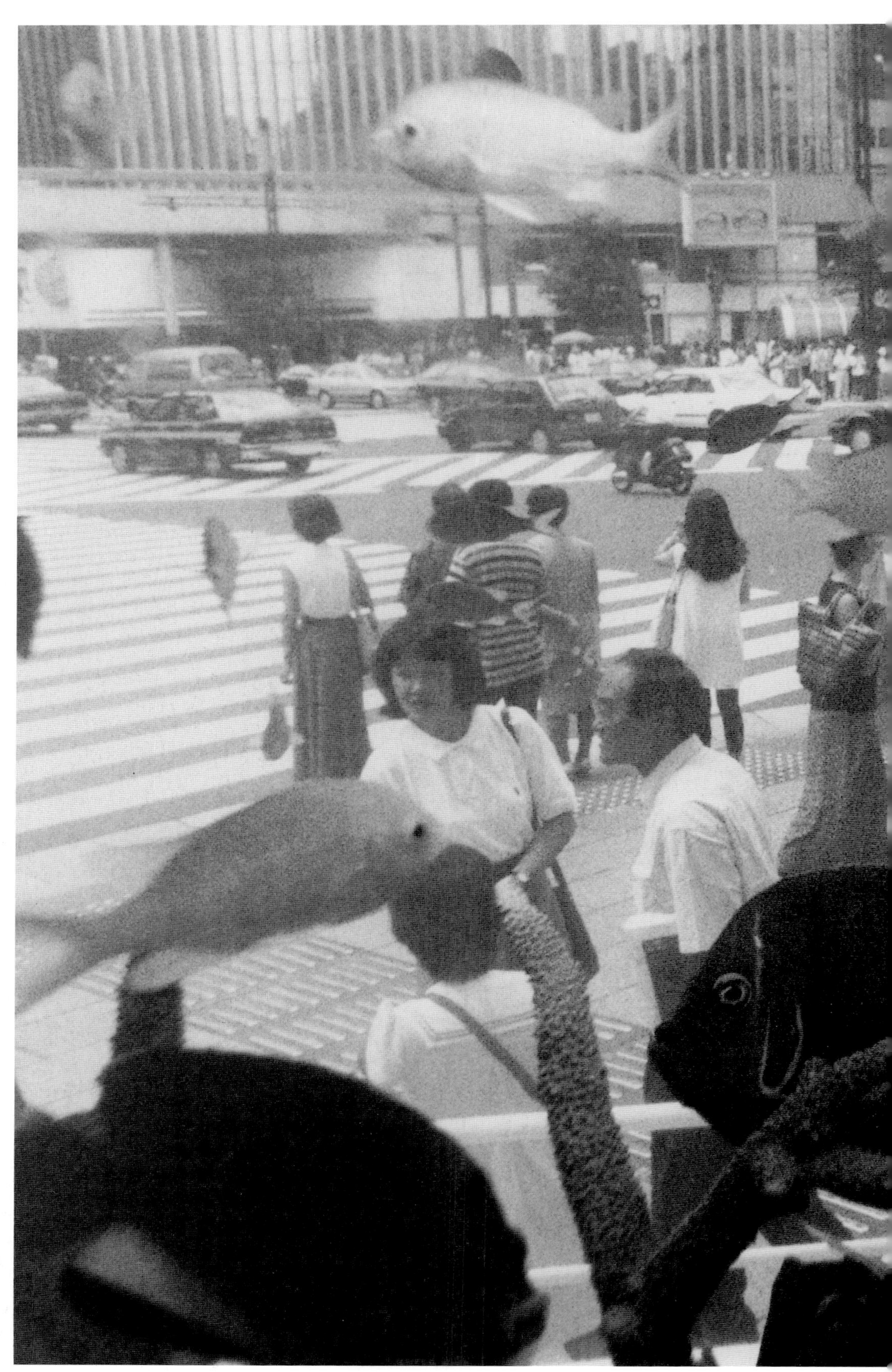

TOKYO, Japan,
23 July 1995
**Exhibition
of tropical fish**
A fish-eye view.

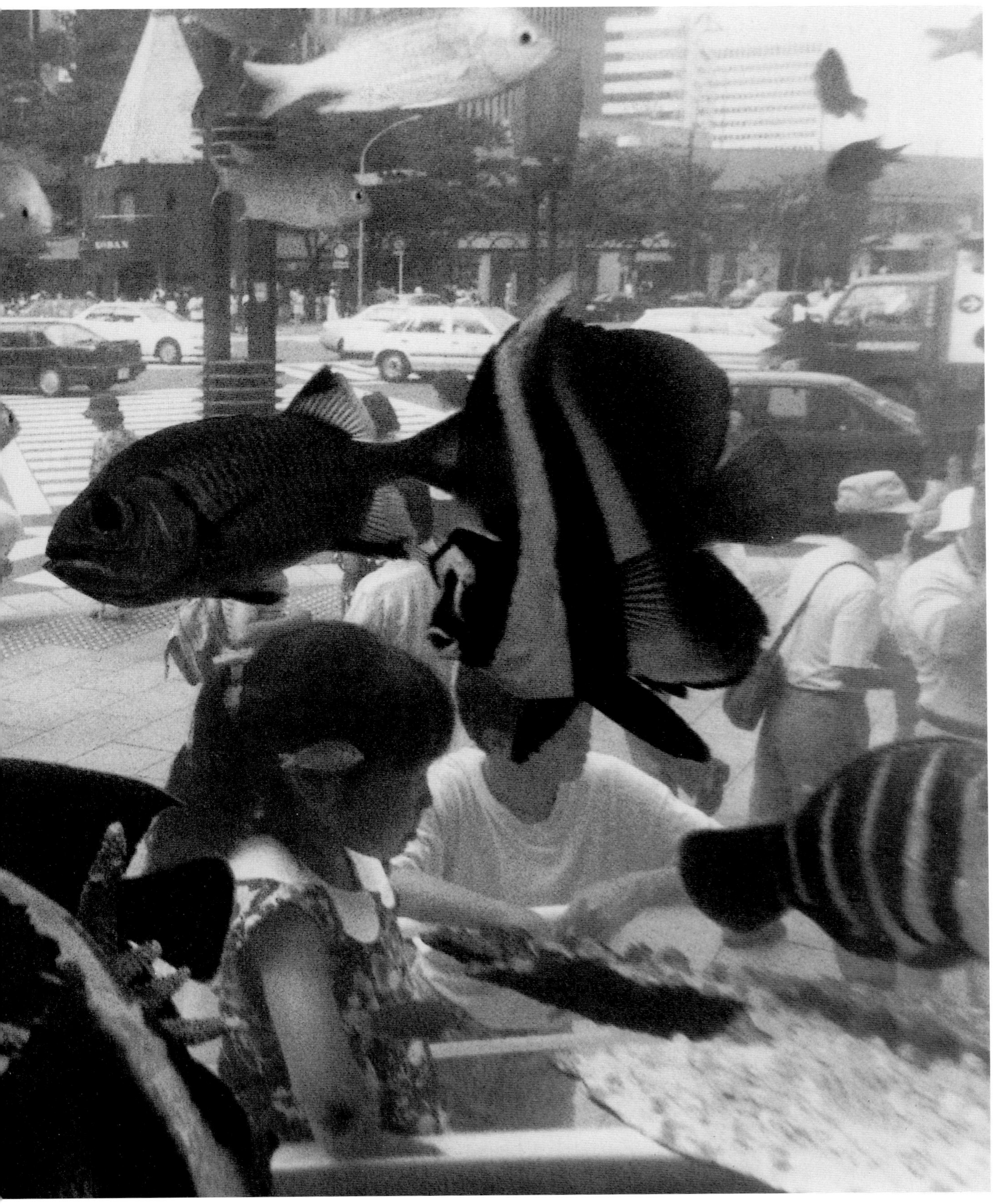

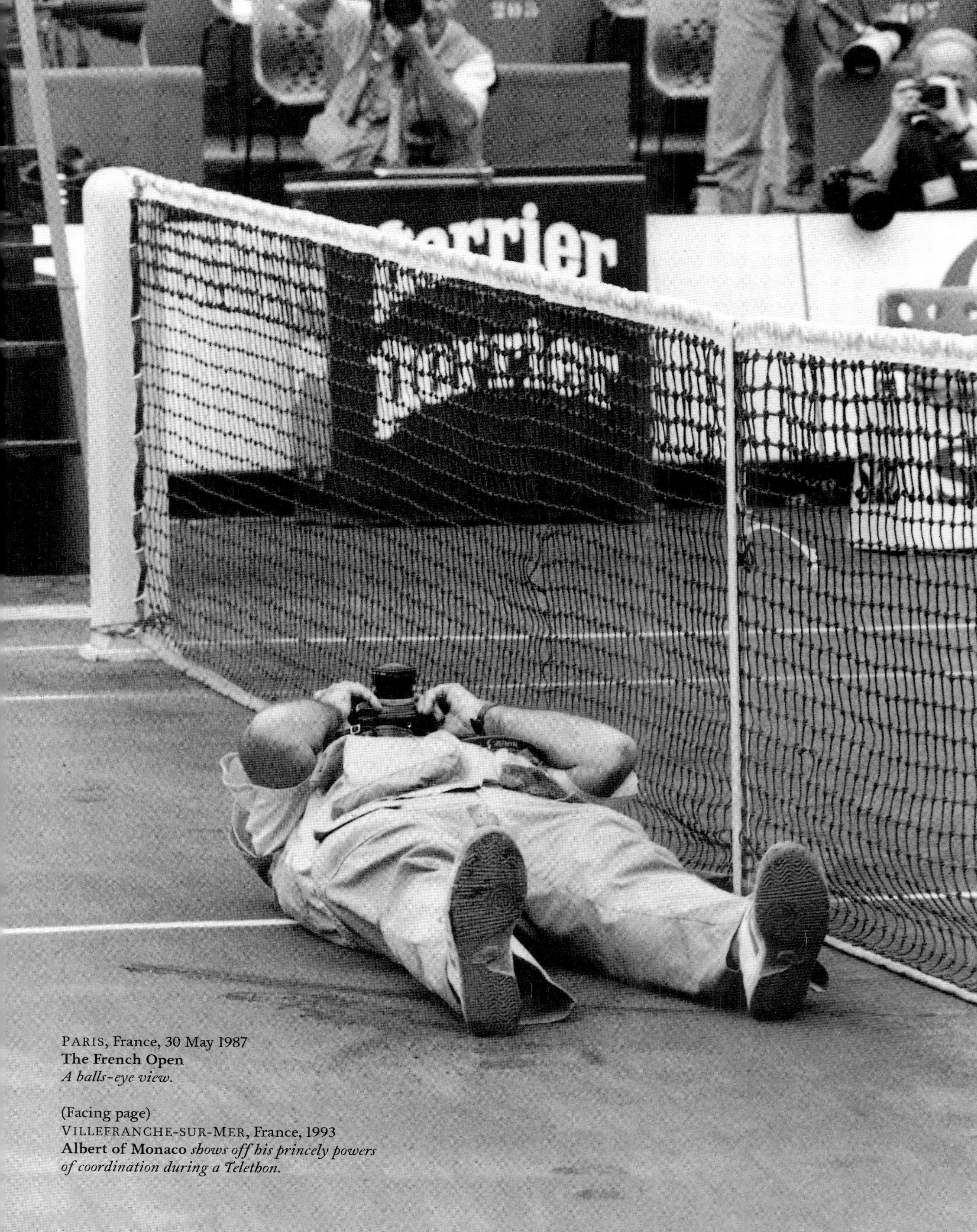

PARIS, France, 30 May 1987
The French Open
A balls-eye view.

(Facing page)
VILLEFRANCHE-SUR-MER, France, 1993
Albert of Monaco *shows off his princely powers
of coordination during a Telethon.*

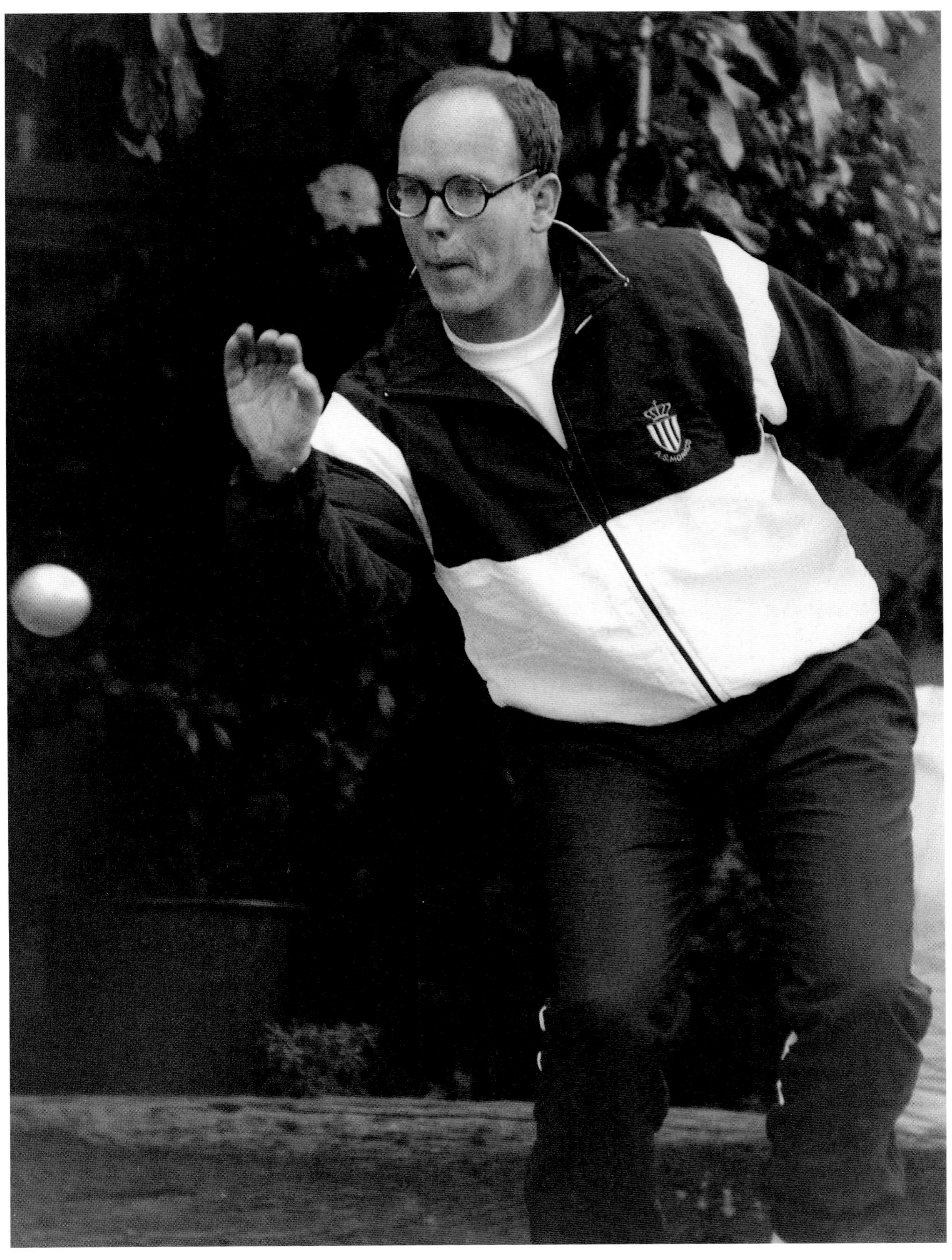

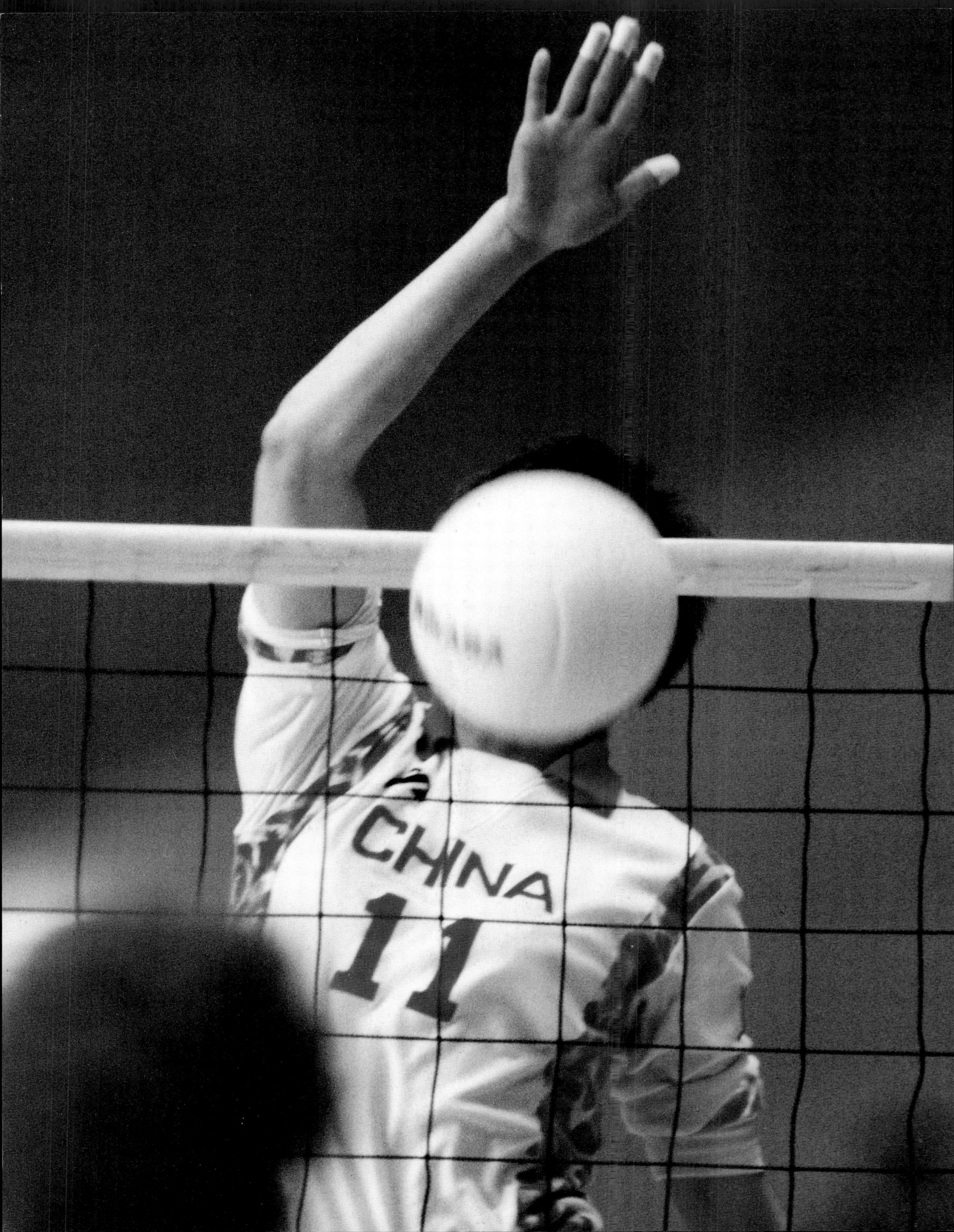

CHINA
11

(Left) TOKYO, Japan, 3 November 1995. **Volleyball World Cup**. *The game that makes you lose your head.*

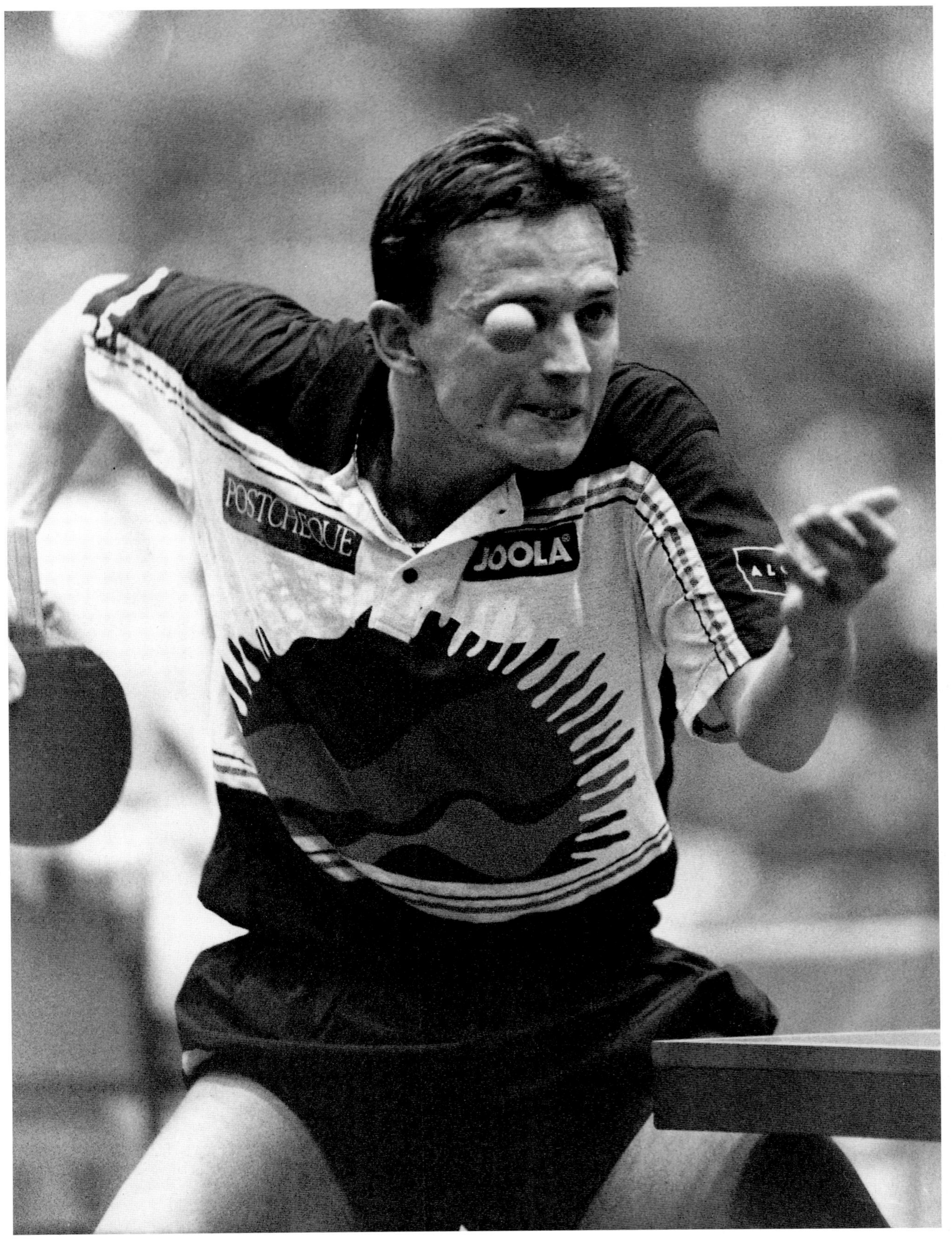

TIANJIN, China, 4 May 1995. **World Table Tennis Championships**. *The trick is not to lose sight of the ball . . .*

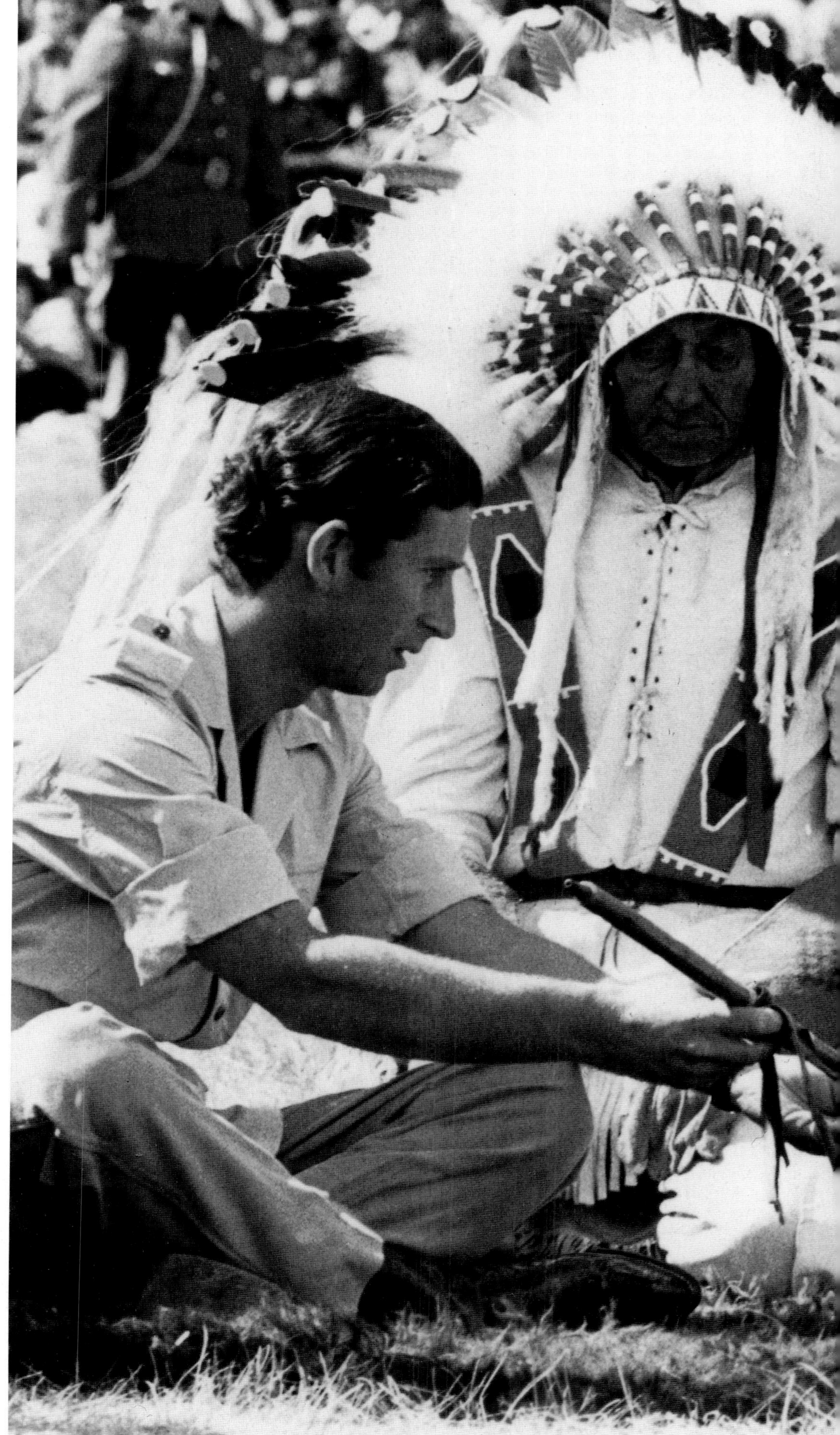

BLACKFOOT CROSSING,
Alberta, Canada,
28 July 1977
**Commemoration of the
signing of a treaty
between
the British Crown
and the Blackfoot
Indians**
*Prince Charles,
with rather more hair
to lose then than
he has now,
seems to be in no fear of
being scalped as he accepts
the peace pipe.*

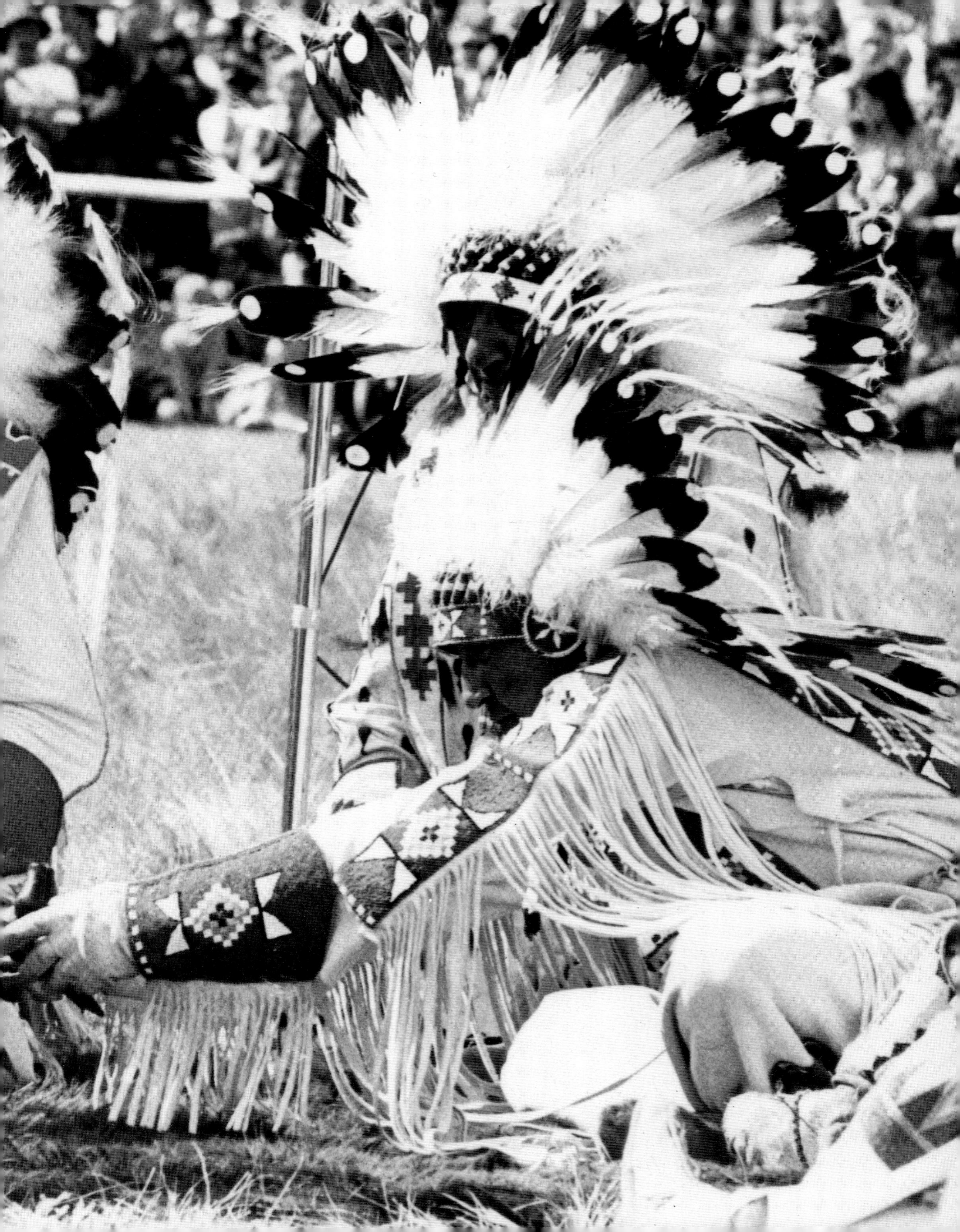

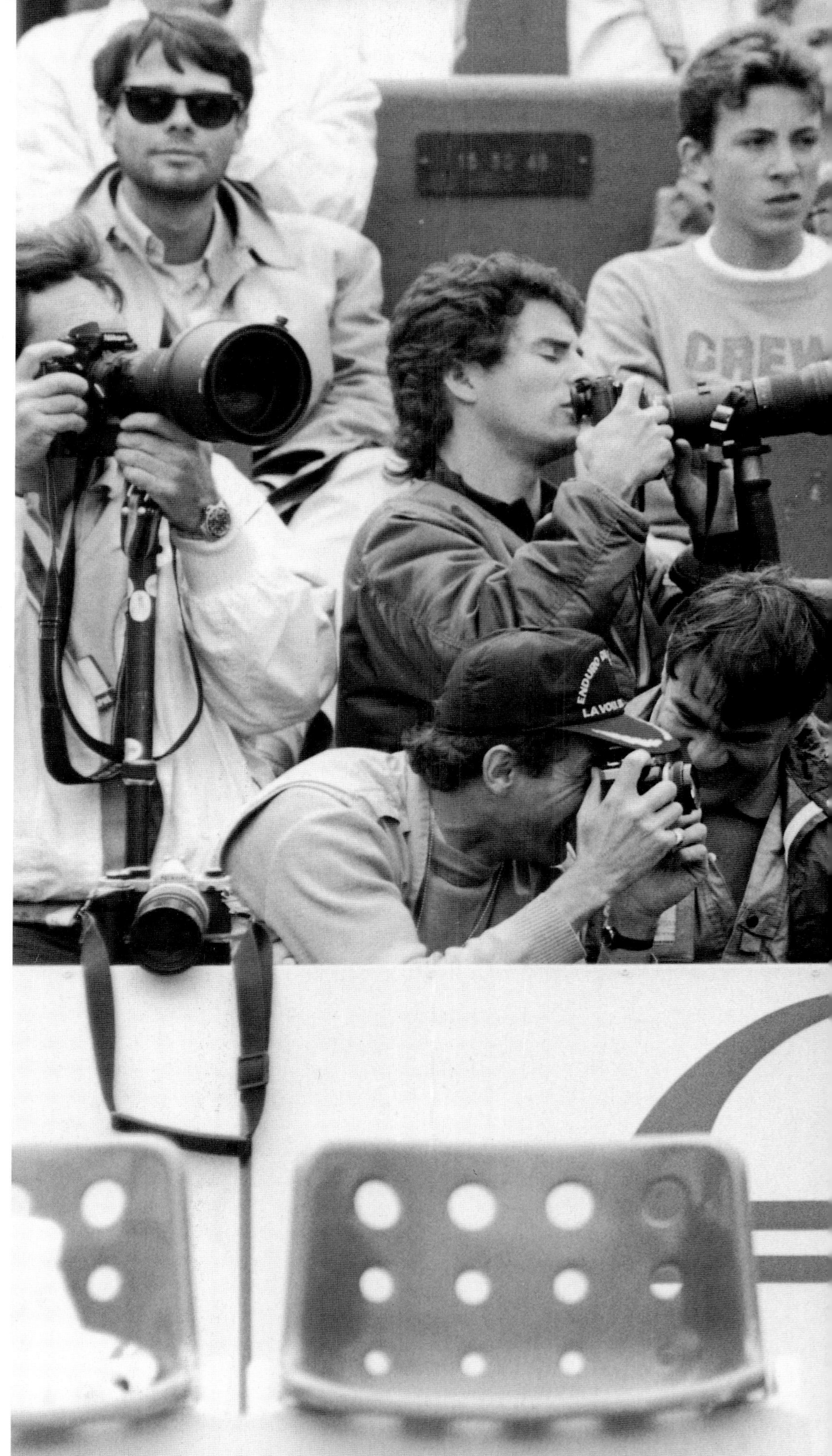

PARIS, France,
5 June 1986
The French Open
*Some use zoom lenses,
others use their
imagination.*

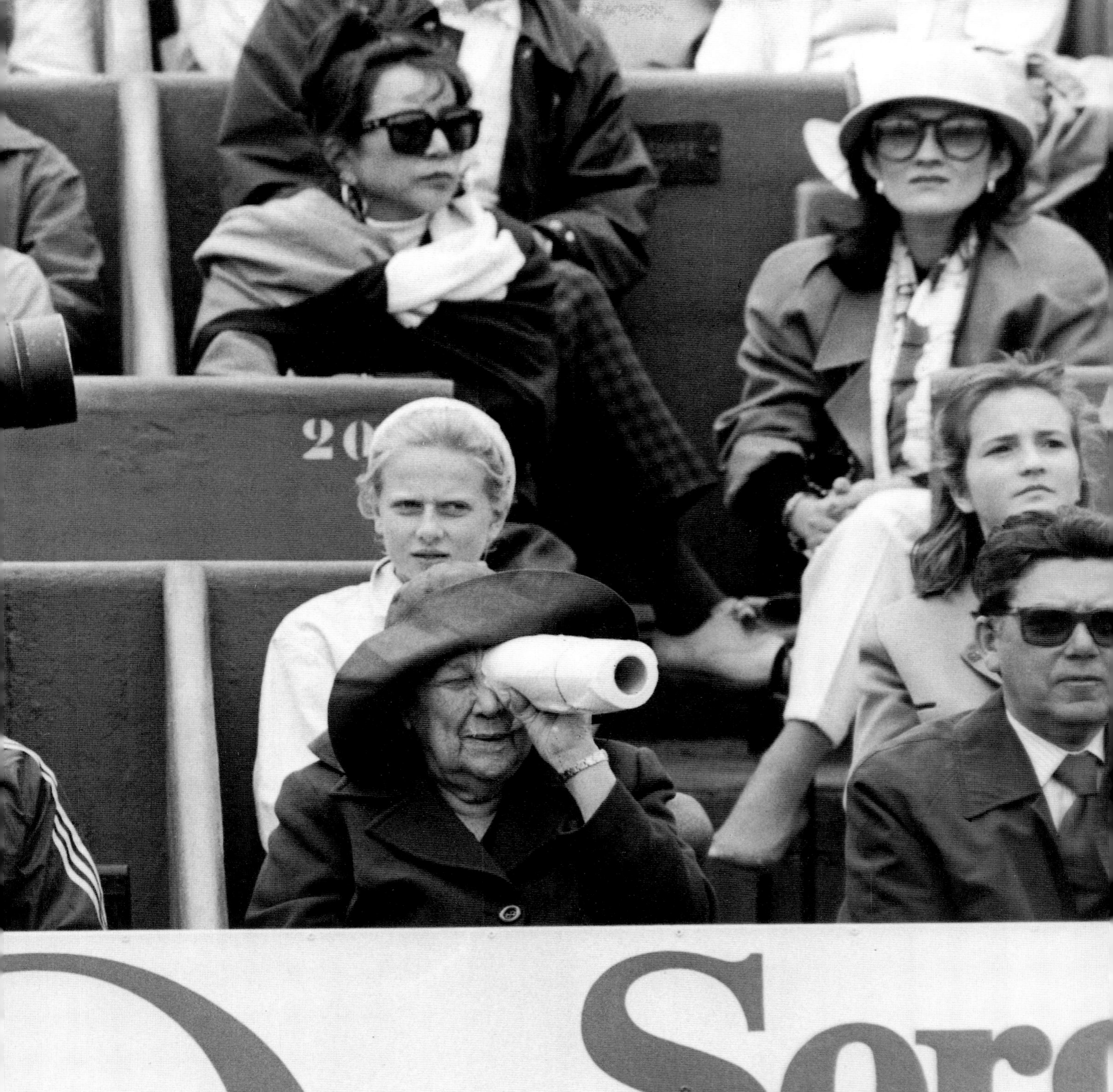
2
Serg
Tac

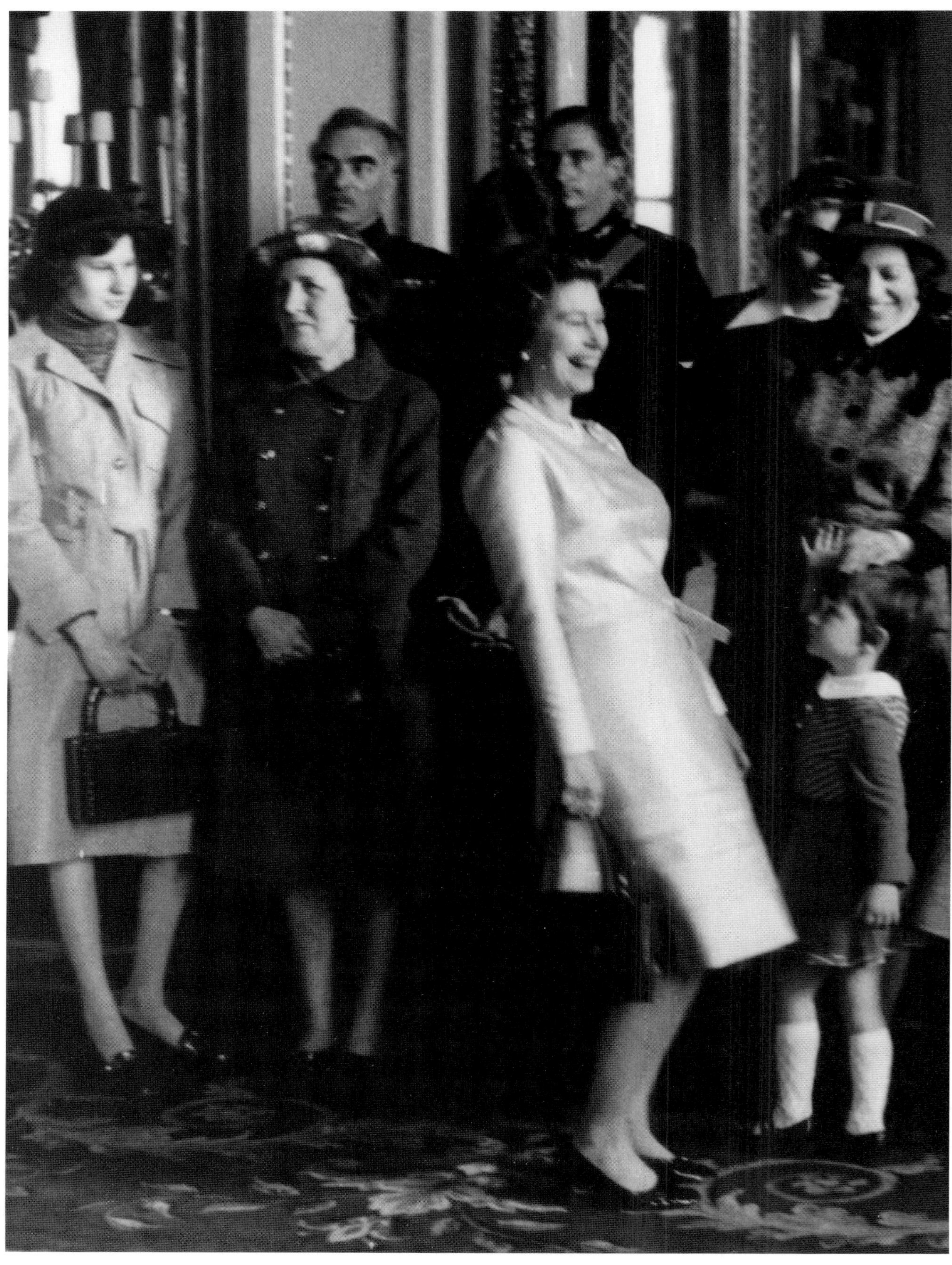

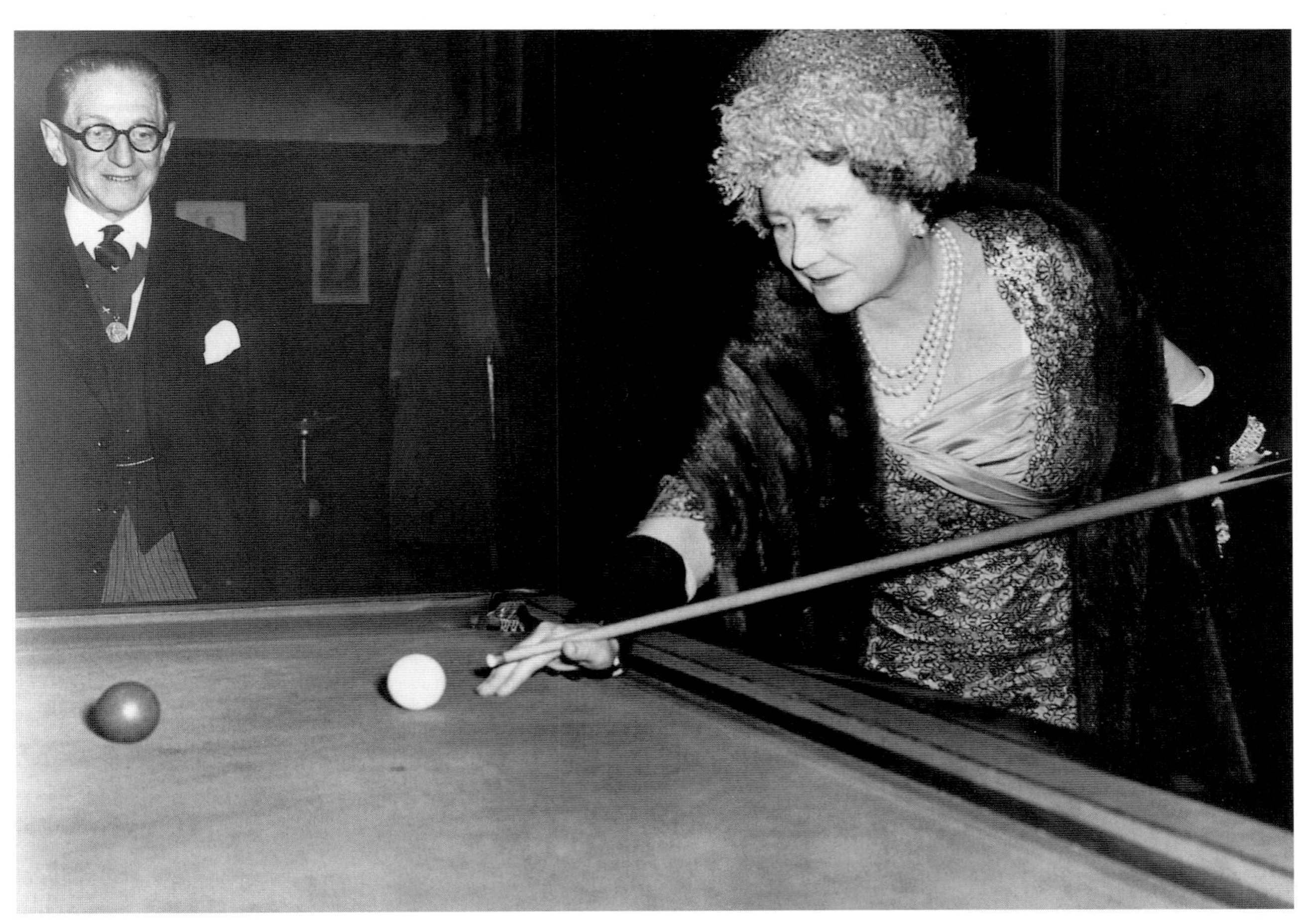

LONDON, Great Britain, 26 November 1974
Reception at Buckingham Palace
Sadly, the Queen has not had so much to laugh about recently.

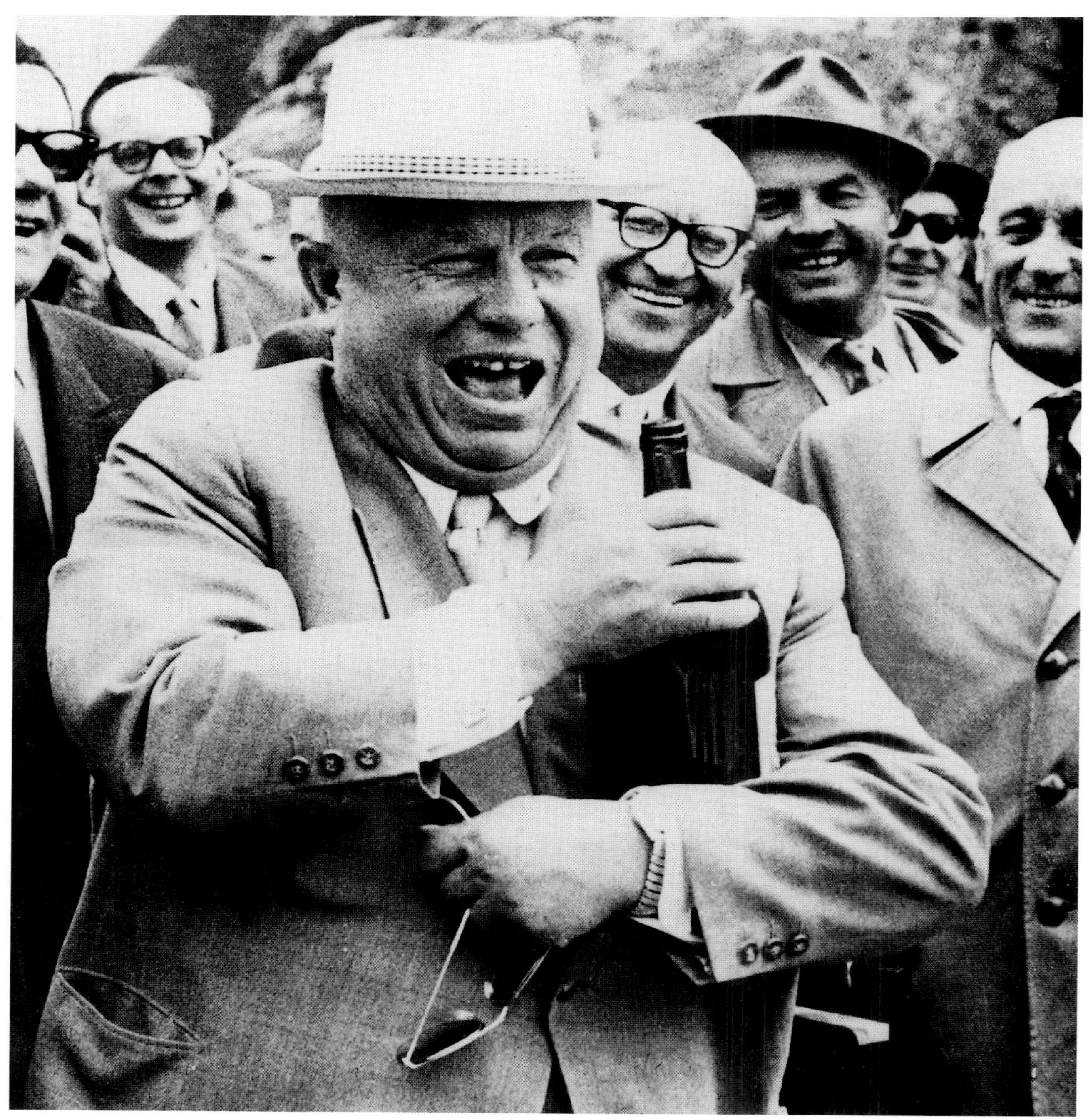

Khrushchev, 1960 . . .

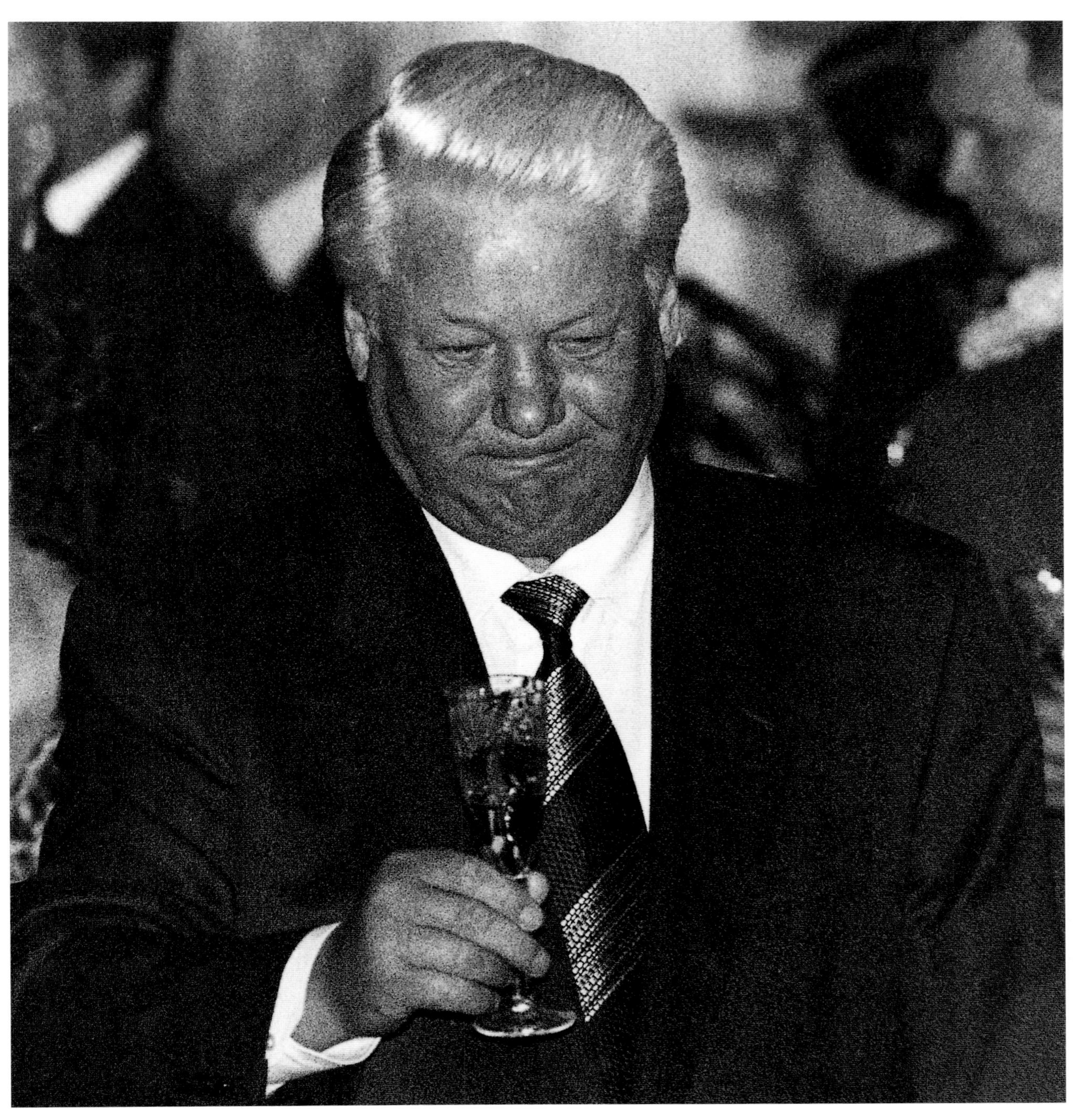

Yelstsin, 1995
**More than 30 years separates these pictures
of Nikita Khrushchev and Boris Yeltsin,**
but in Russia tradition dies hard.

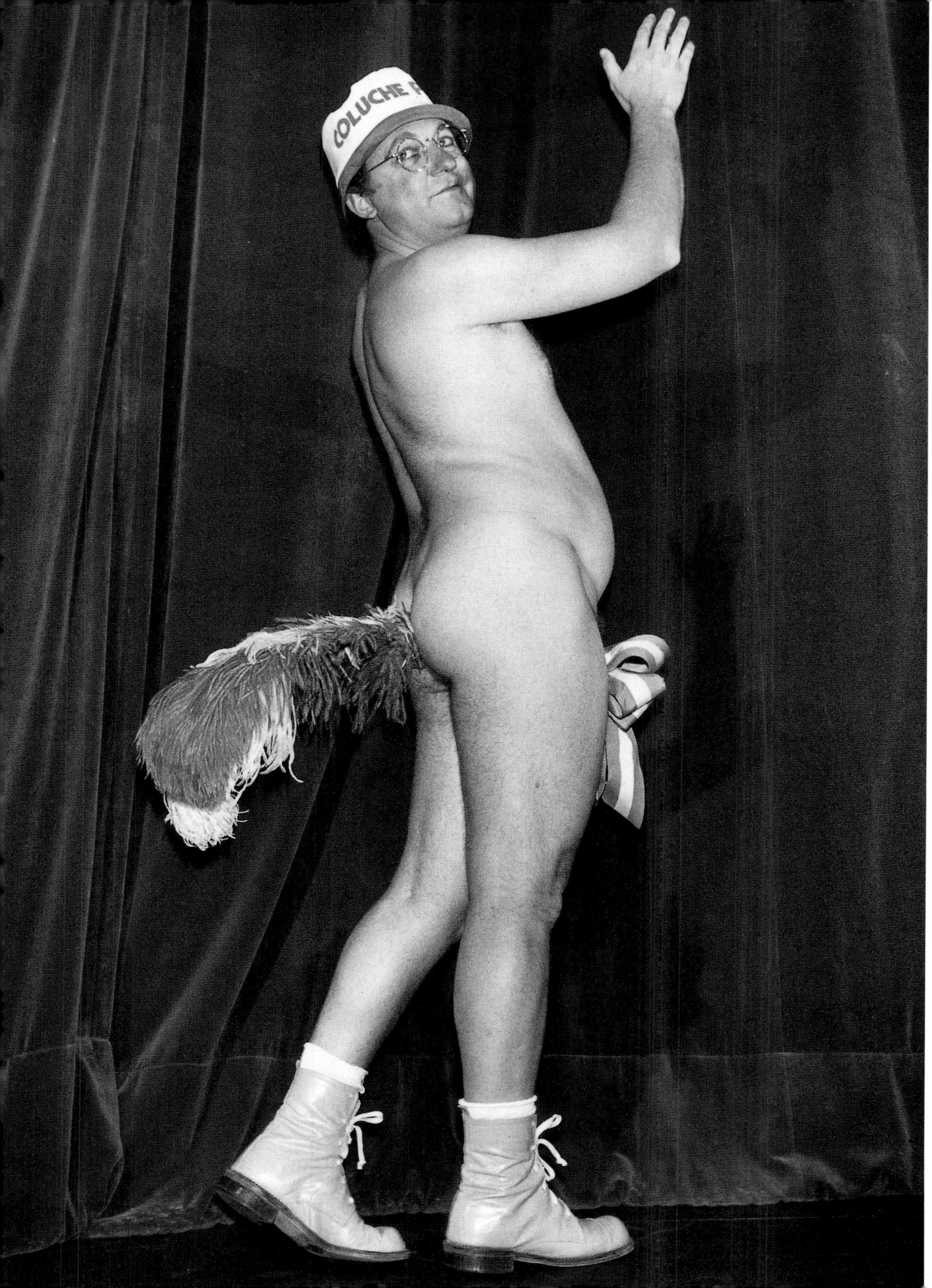
COLUCHE P

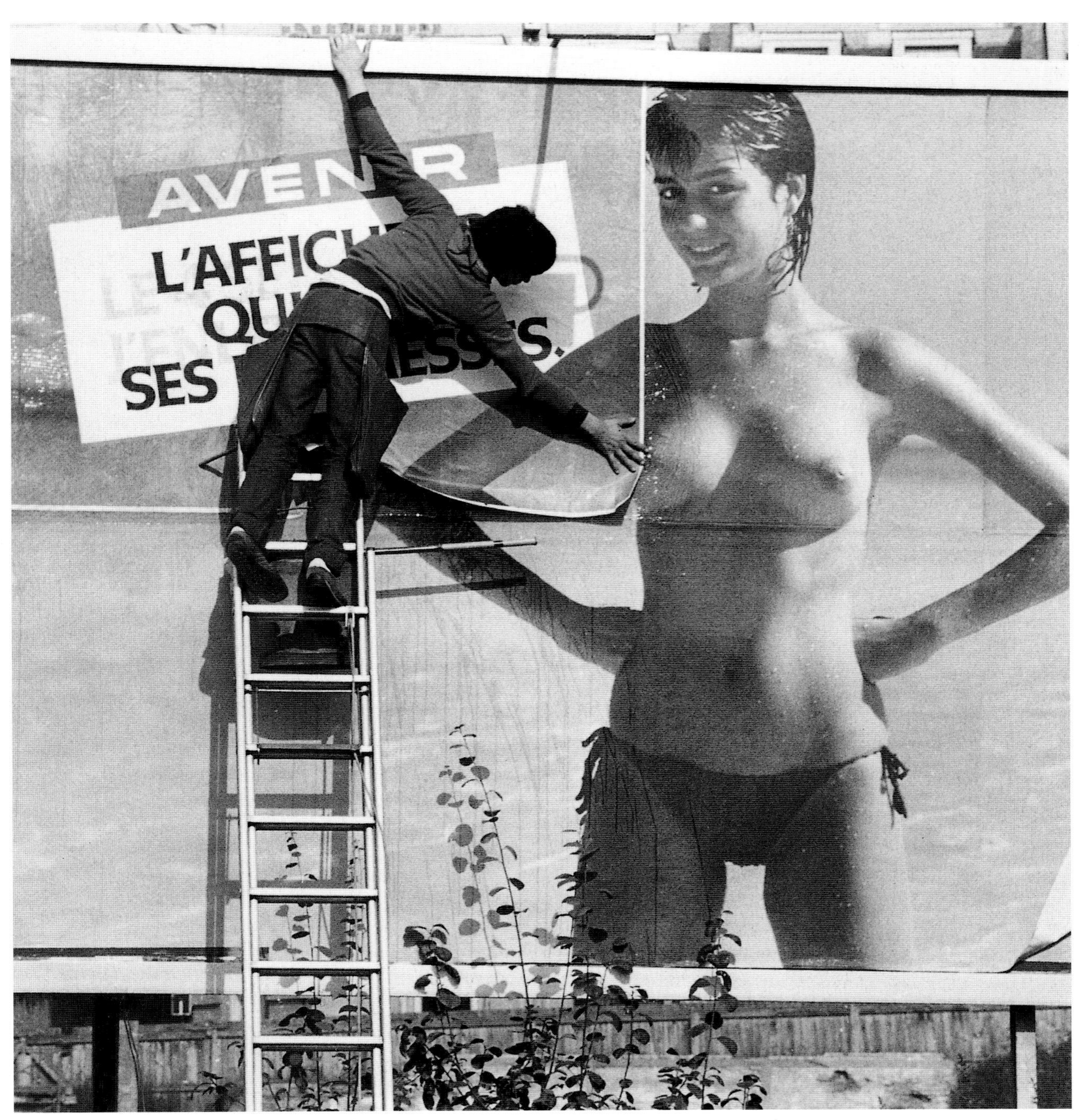

PARIS, France, 4 September 1981
Later she took off the bottom . . .
One of France's most famous advertisements
was for a billboard company
"which keeps its promises".

PARIS, France, 2 March 1981
The comedian Coluche stands for president
Coluche exhibits a strong patriotic streak,
by posing as the national symbol of France – a cockerel.

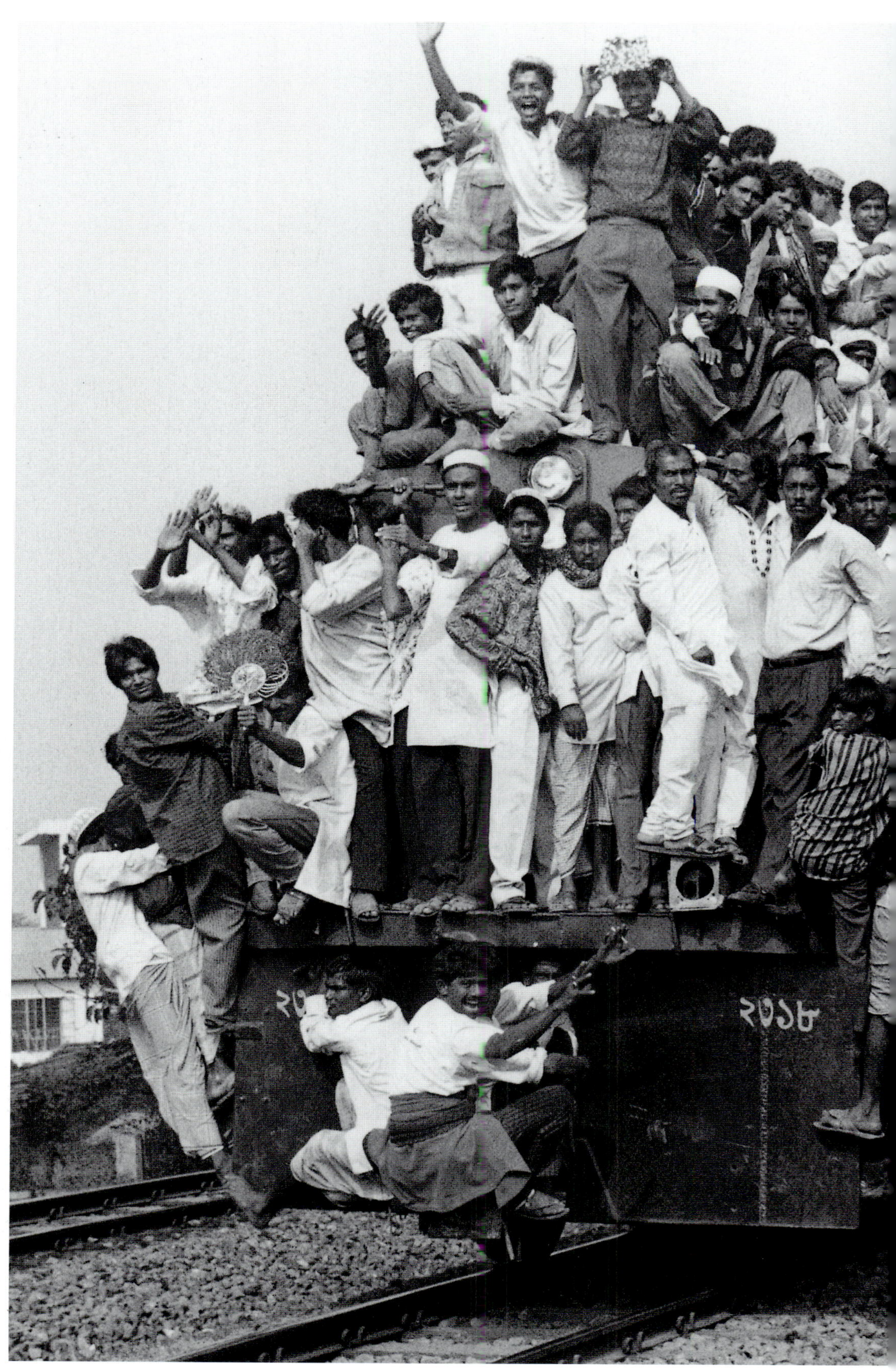

TONGI, Bangladesh,
18 January 1993
**Return from the World
Islamic Congress**
*I did ask for
a window seat,
but this is ridiculous.*

70

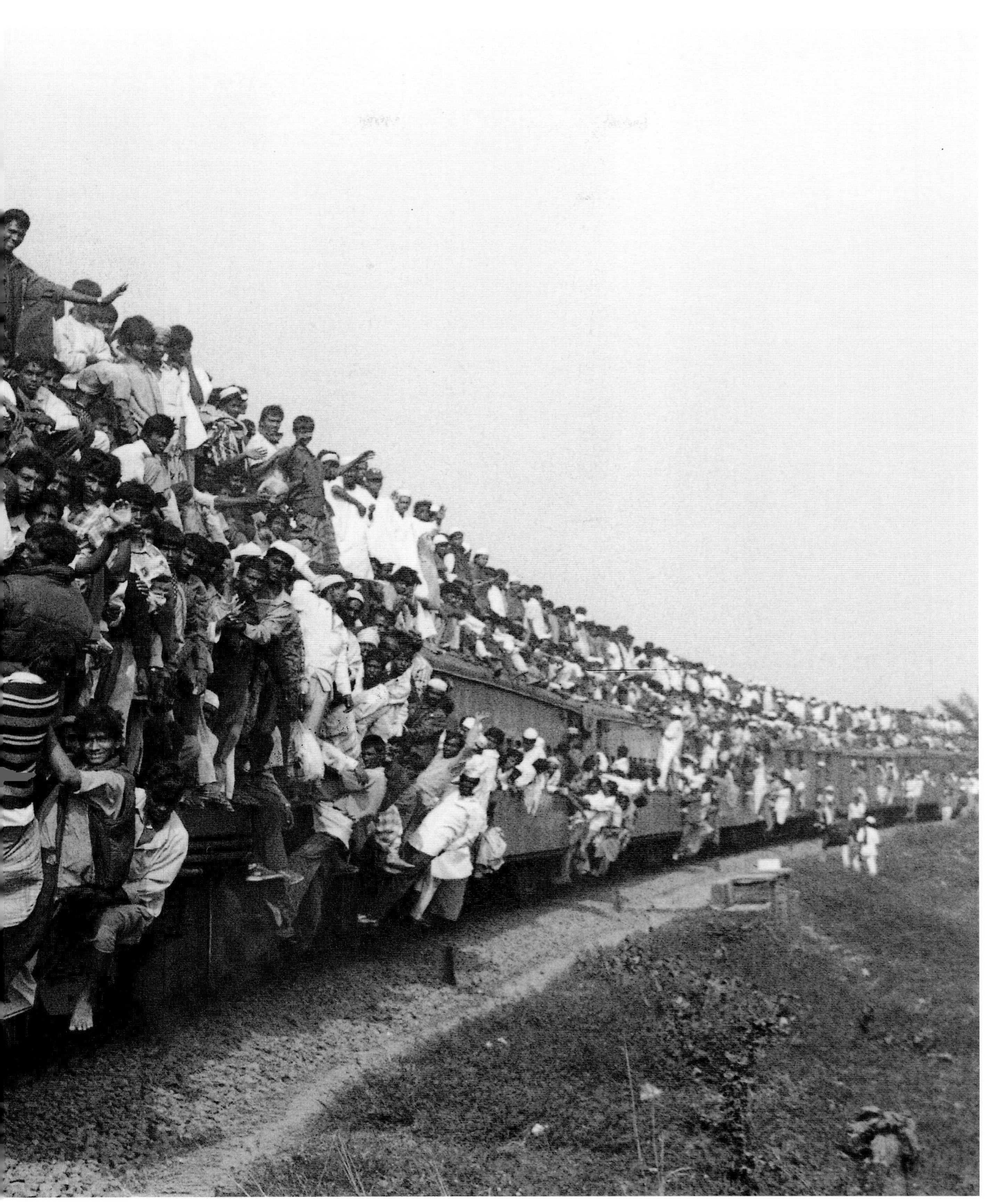

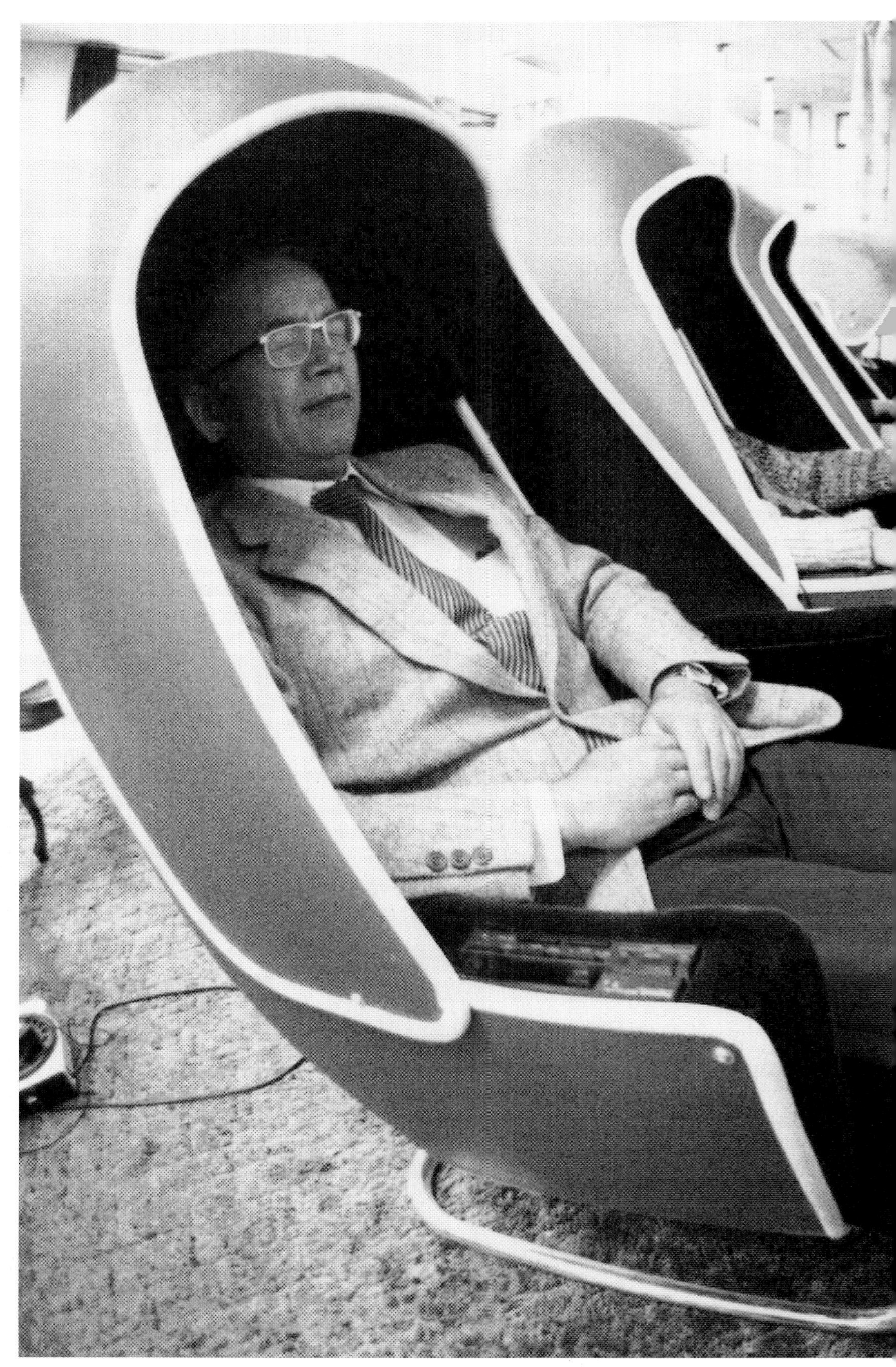

Asian siesta
At last!
All the joys of nature
without the inconvenience
of mosquitos or hay fever!

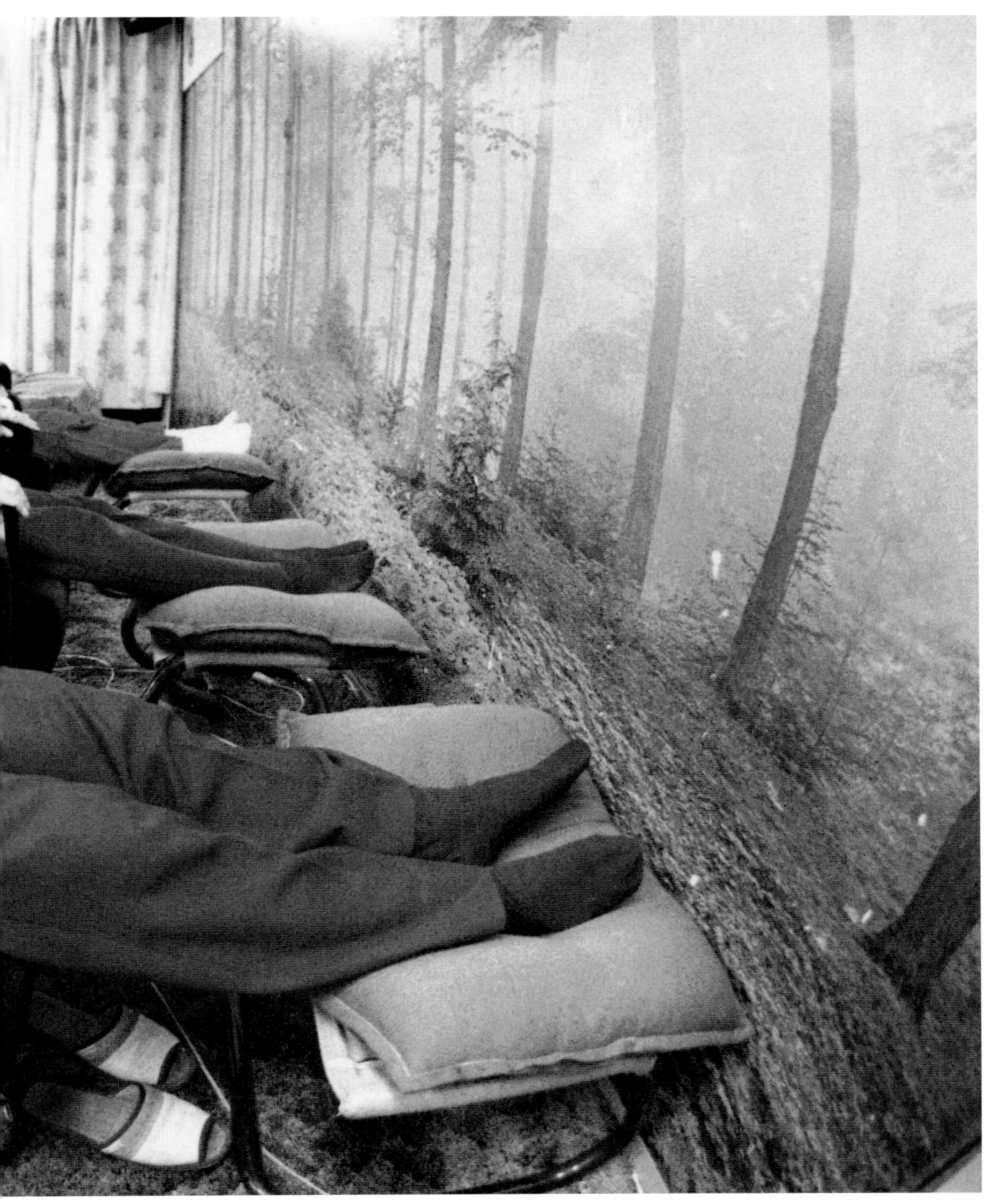

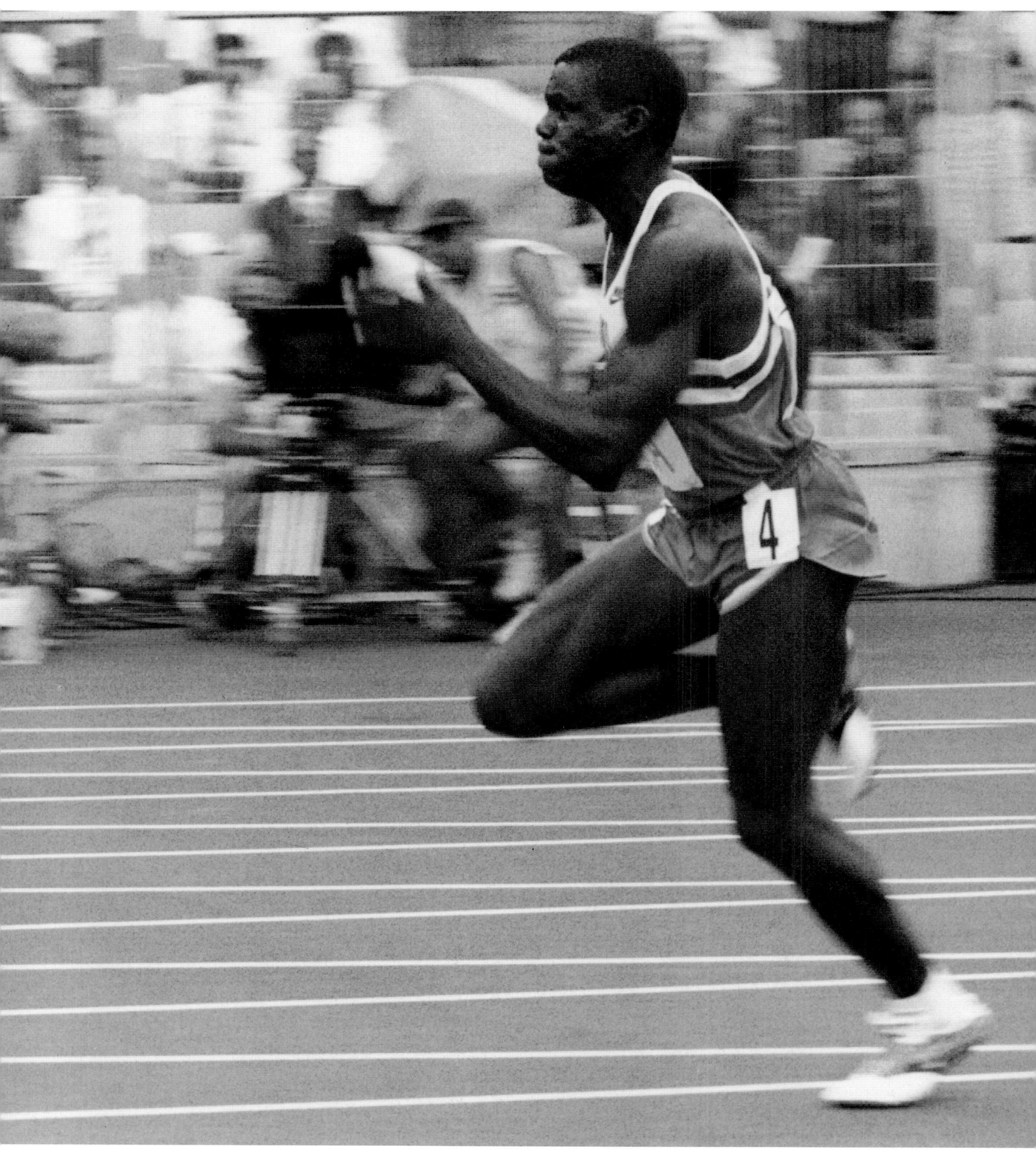

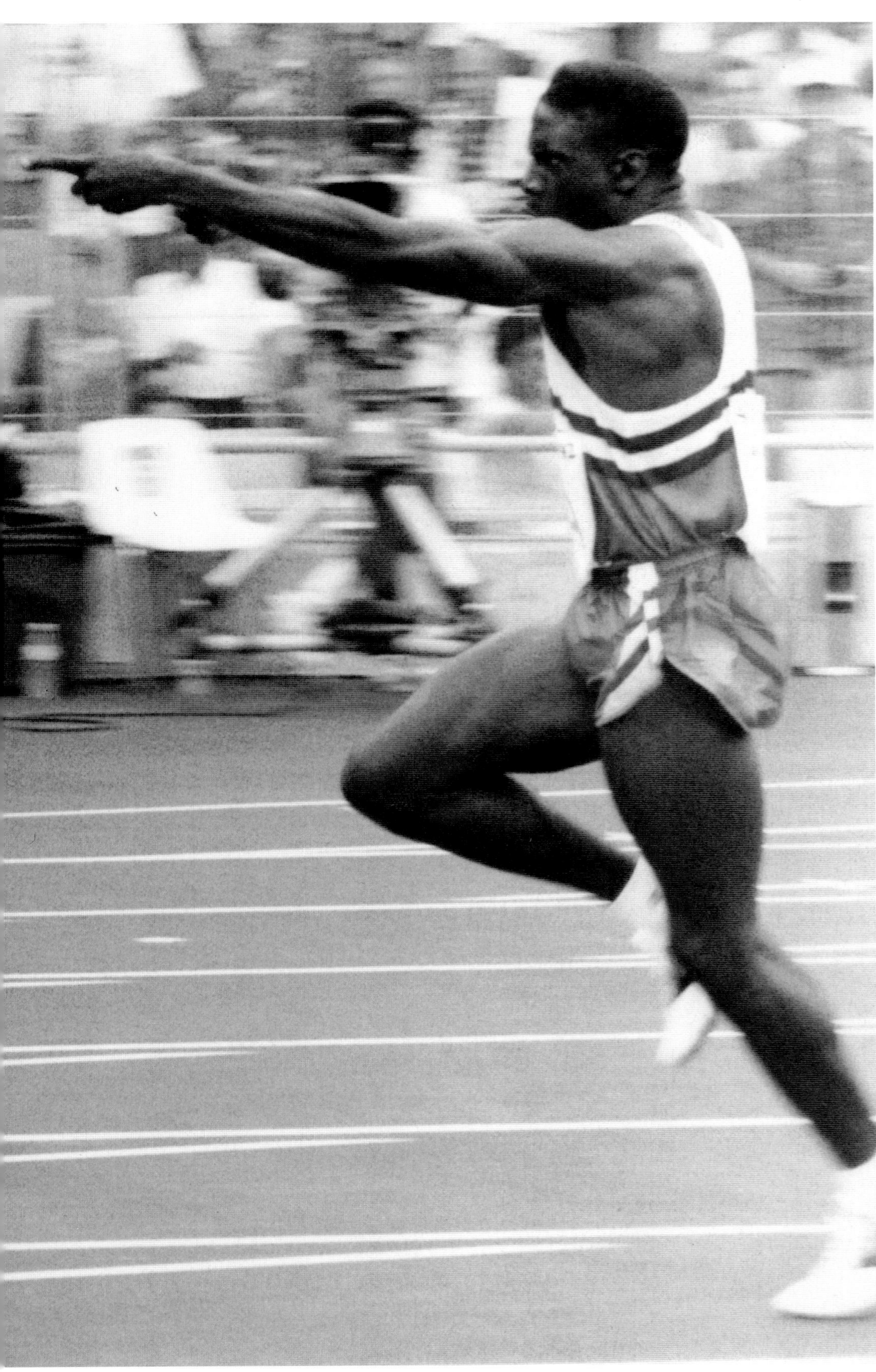

BARCELONA, Spain,
8 August 1992
**Victory for
the Americans
in the 4 x 100 metres
relay: Carl Lewis
and Dennis Mitchell.**
Faster or I'll shoot!

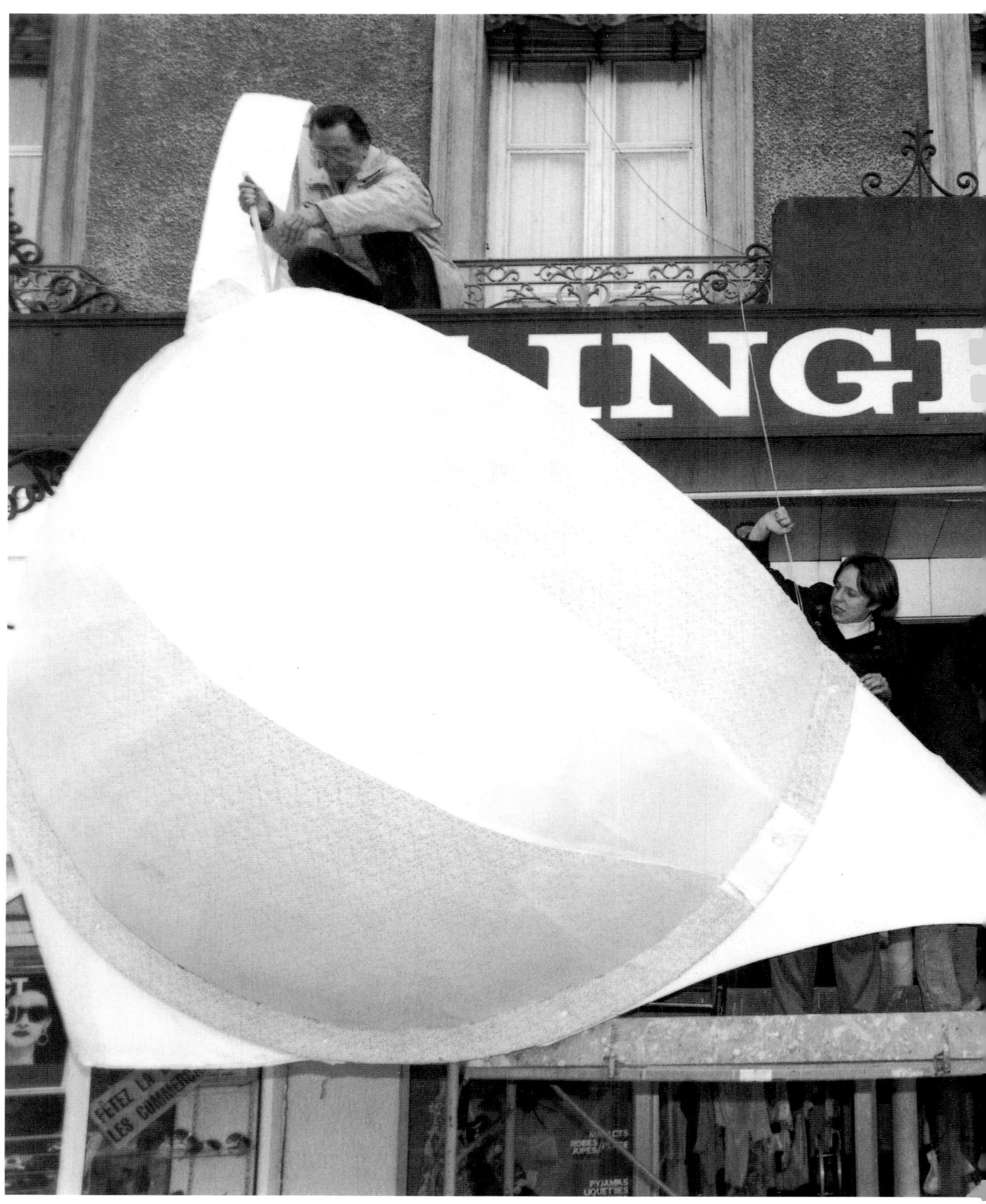

INGE
FÊTEZ LA
LES COMMERÇ
ROBES
JUPES
PYJAMAS
LIQUETTES

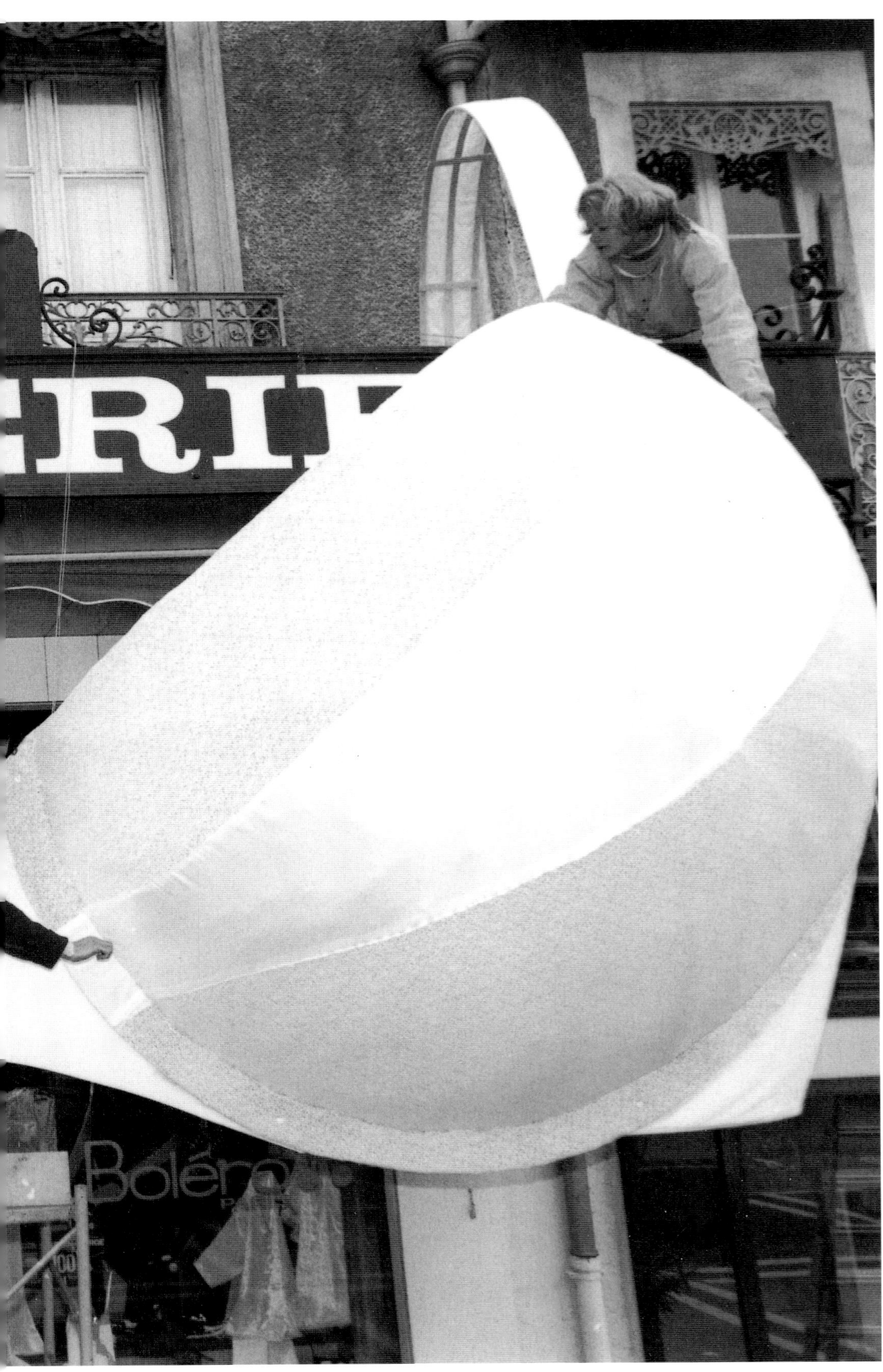

VOIRON, France,
 21 December 1989
**The centenary of
the brassiere**
*One underwear shop
shows a generous degree
of support for the French
lingerie industry.*

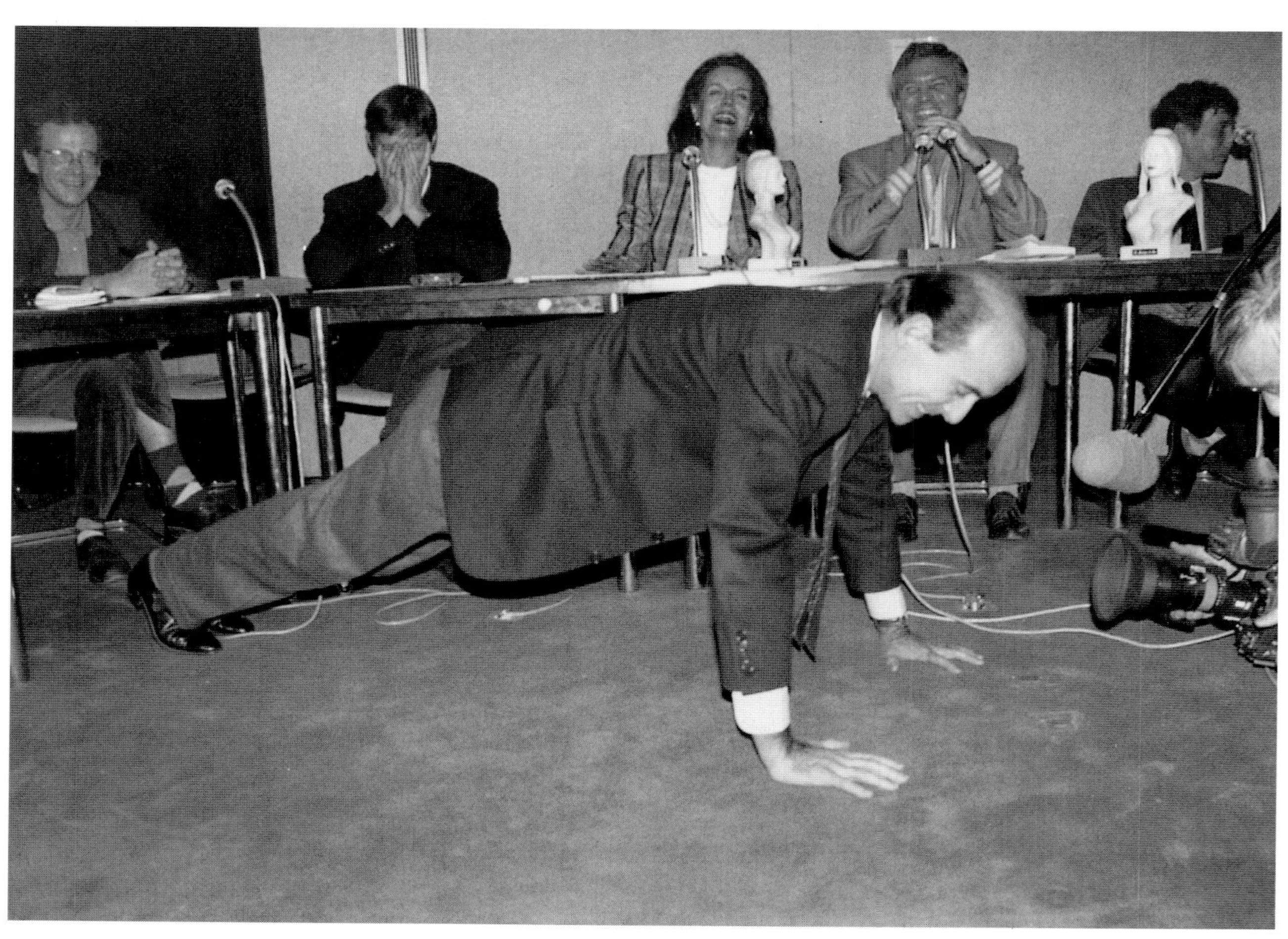

PARIS, France, 21 November 1990
Much to the amusement of assembled journalists,
Alain Juppé shows his fitness for his forthcoming "marriage" to la république.

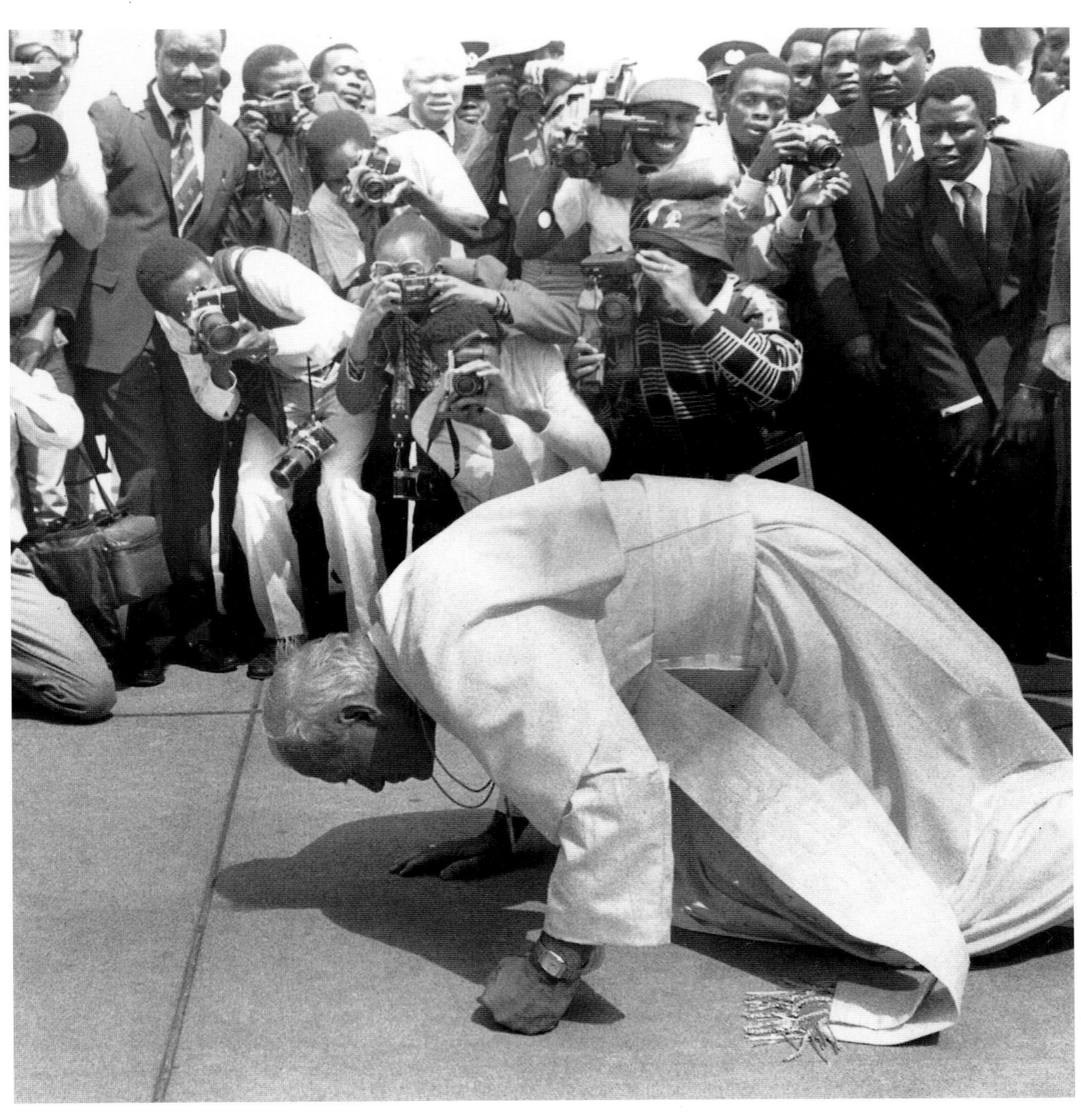

GABORONE, Botswana,
Papal visit
Yuk! Tarmac for breakfast again.

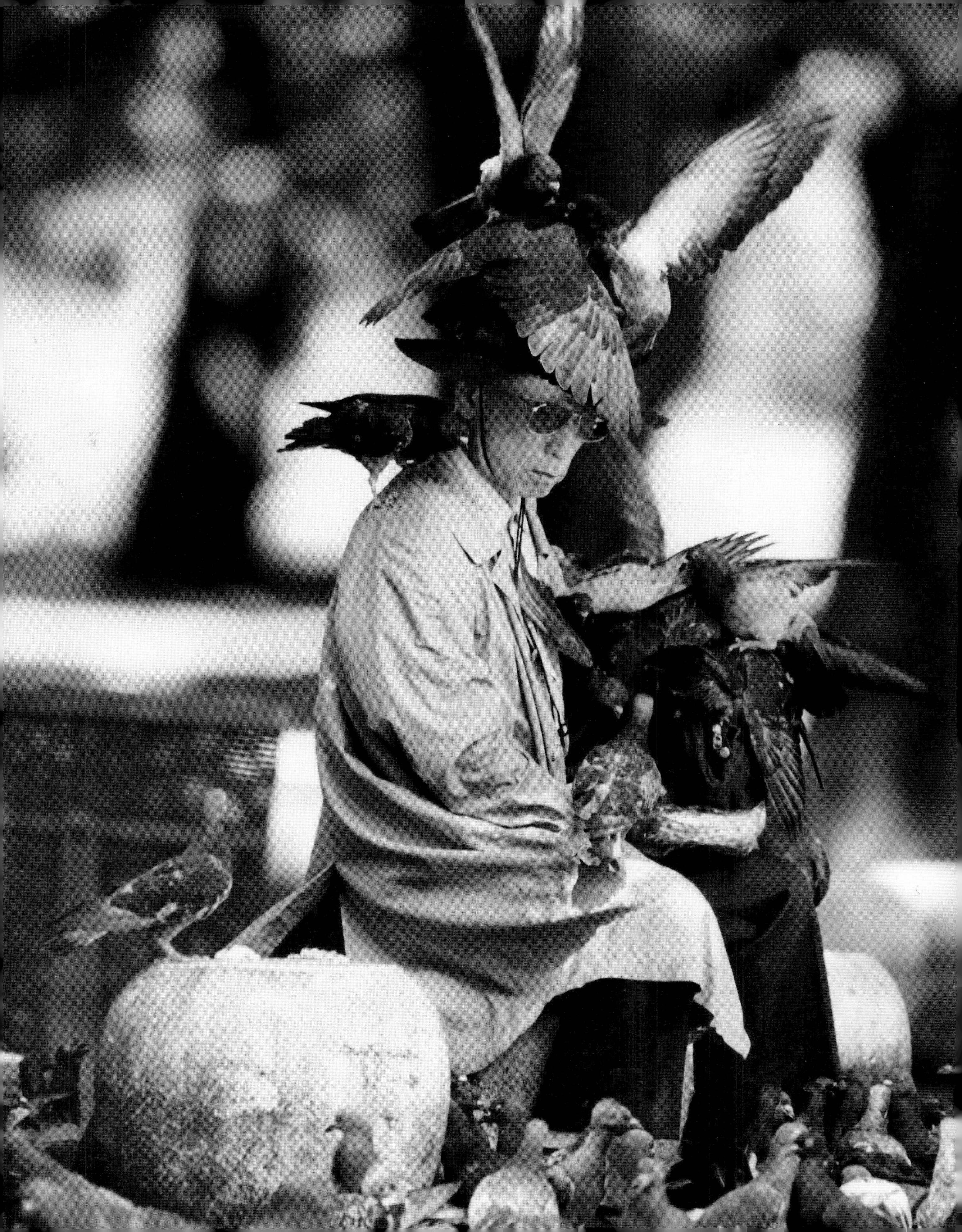

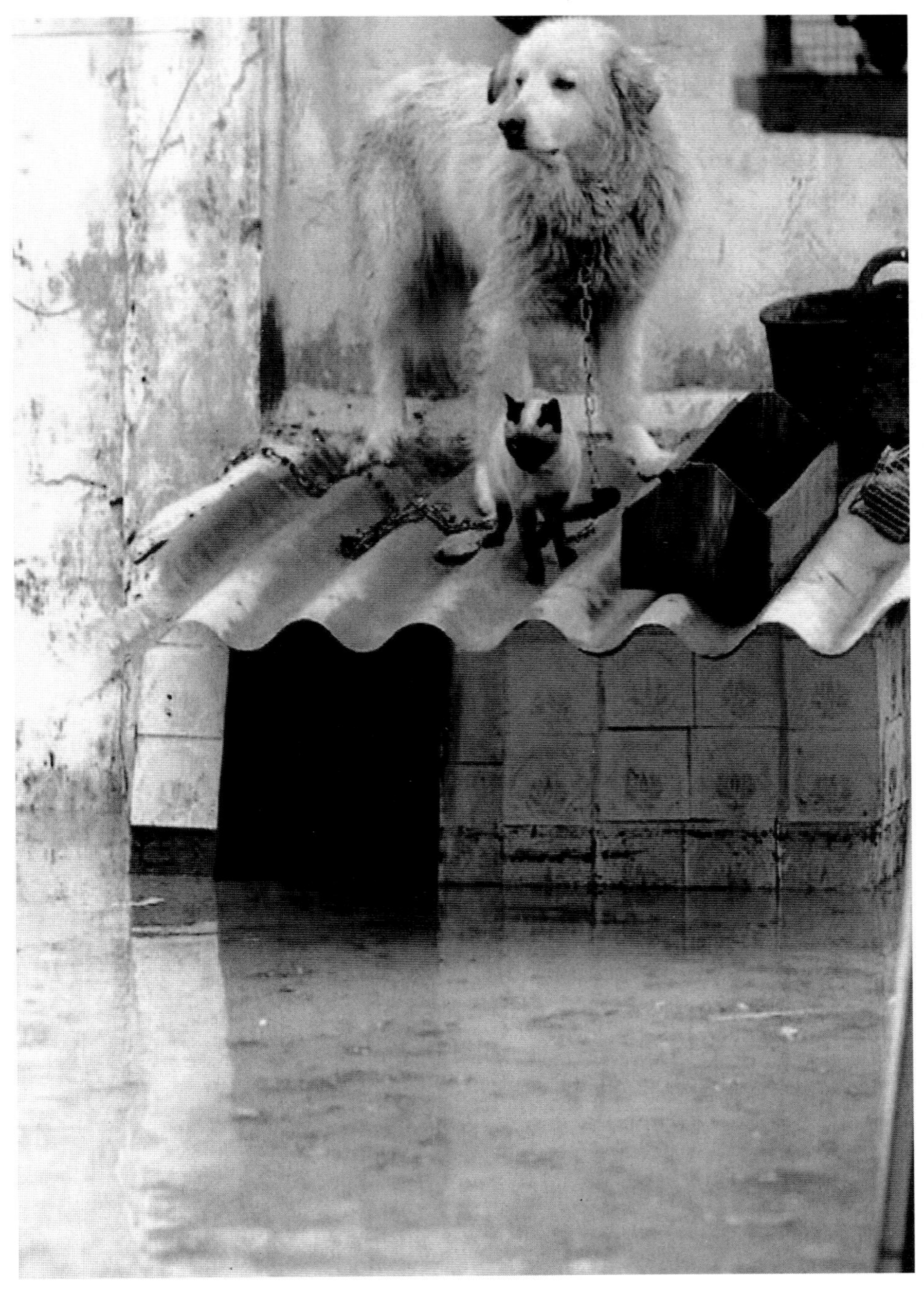

TOKYO, Japan, 24 August 1995
**This man has evidently never seen
Alfred Hitchcock's *The Birds*.**

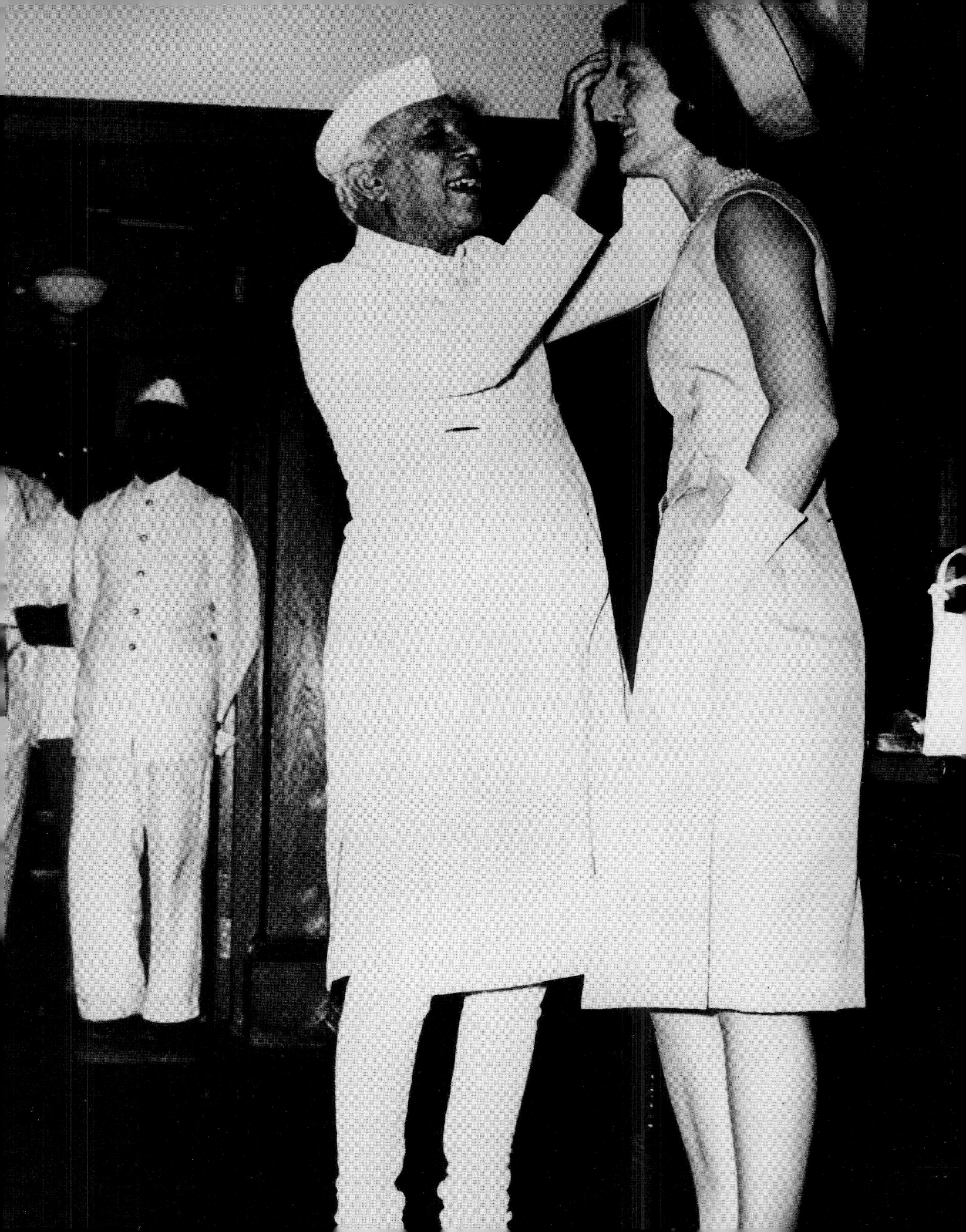

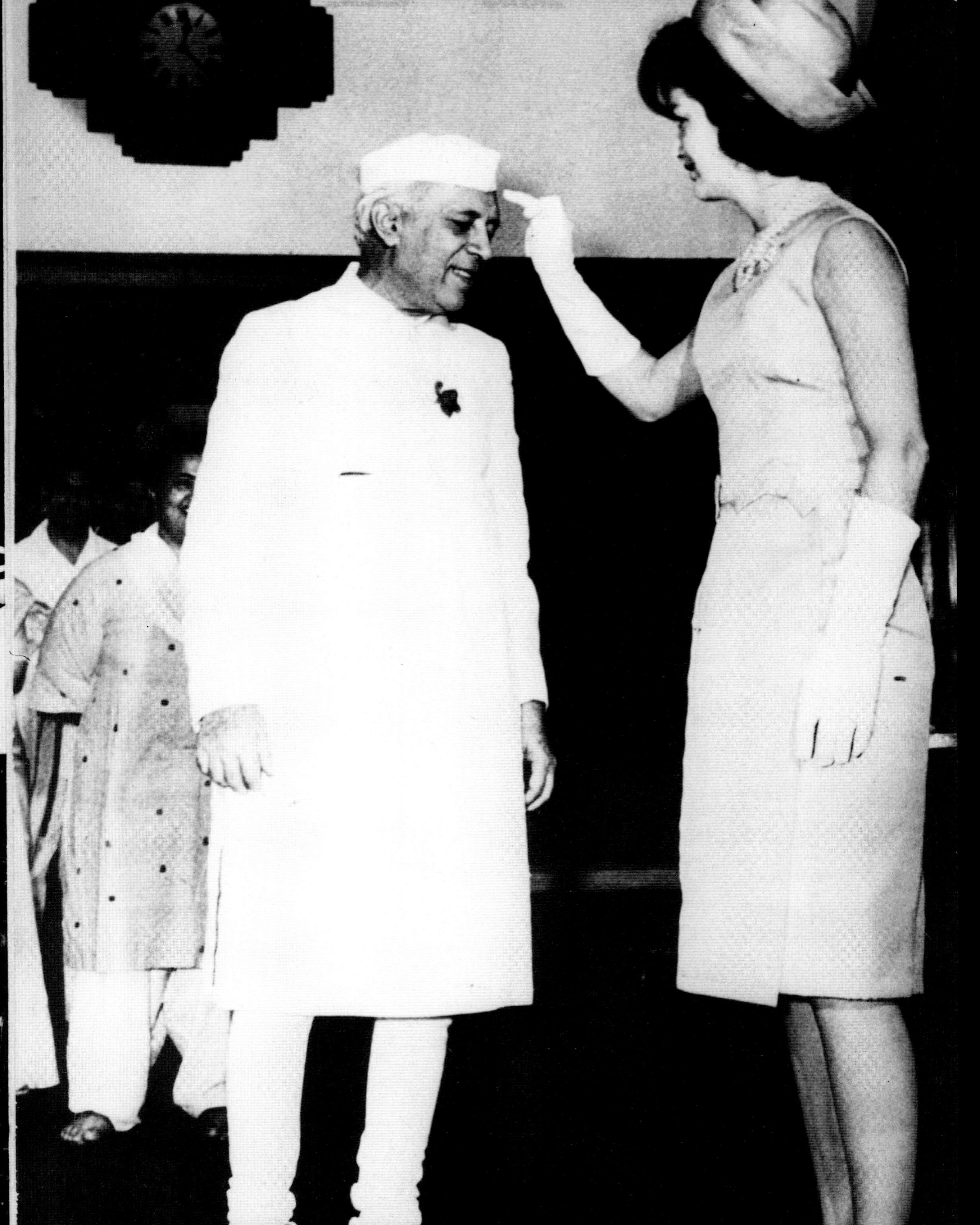

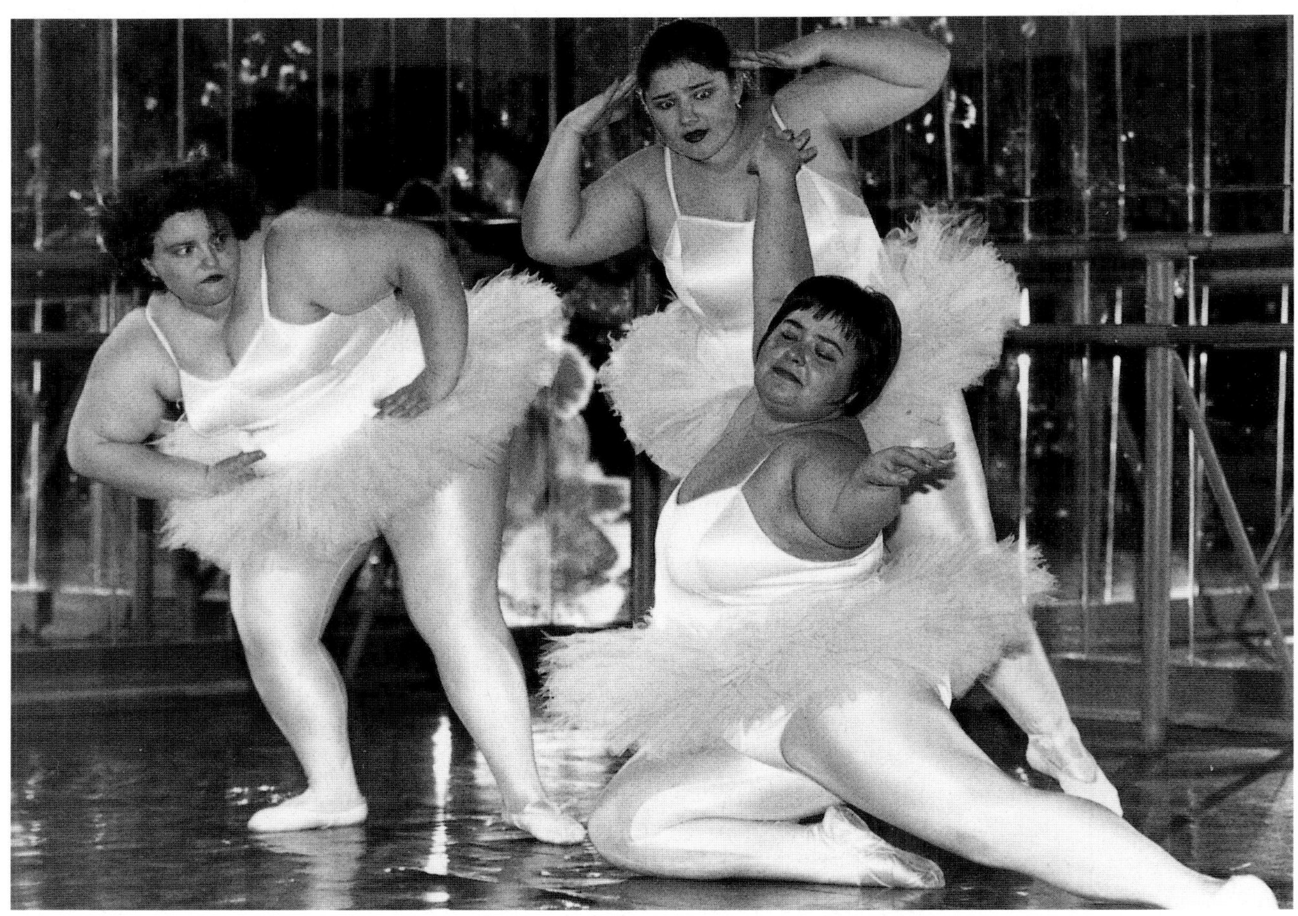

ST PETERSBURG, Russia, 3 May 1995
Swan Lake **at Leningrad Music Hall**
No-one ever said you have to be light on your feet
to wear a tutu . . .

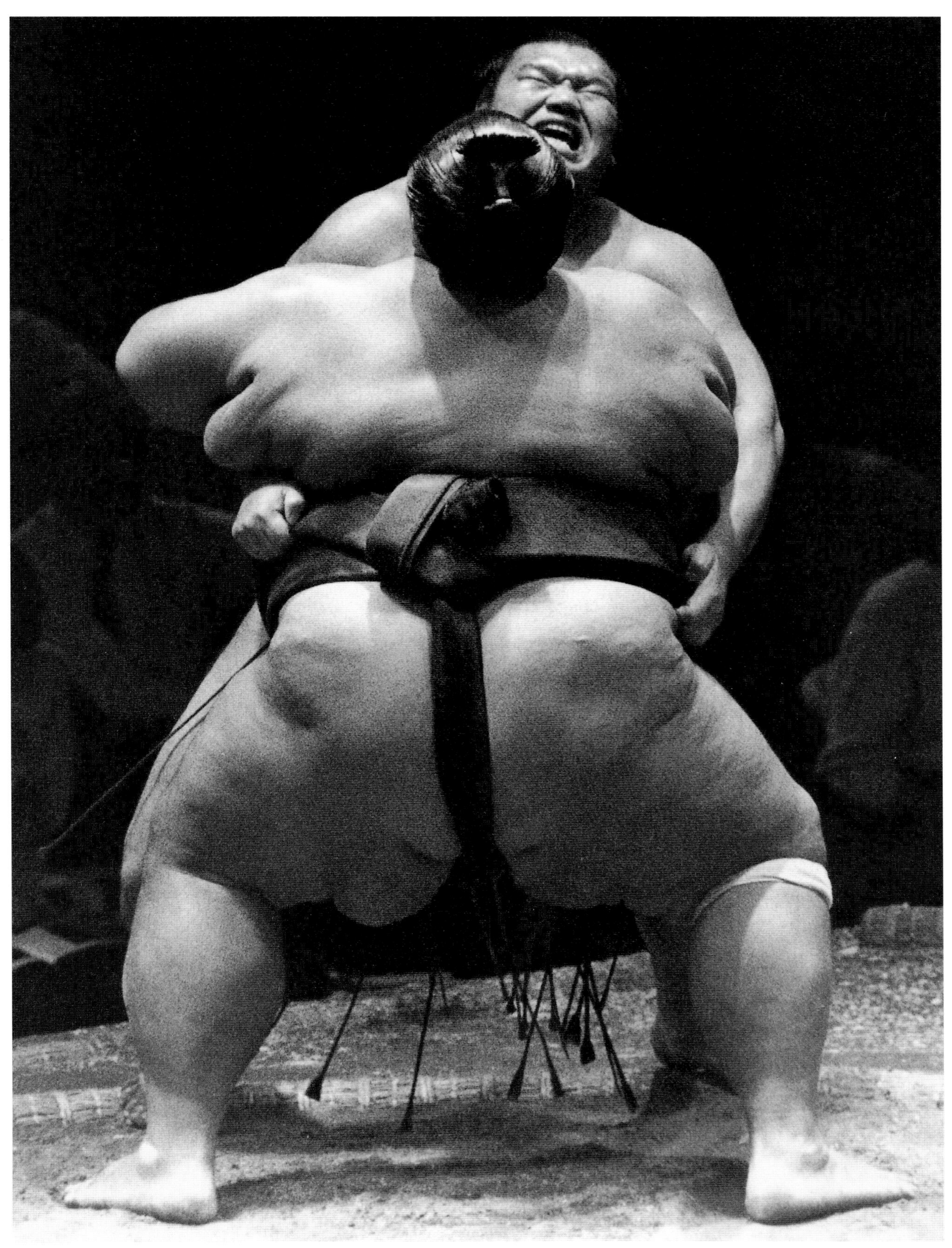

LONDON, Great Britain, 9 October 1991. **The first sumo wrestling tournament outside Japan**
The battle of the bulge takes on new proportions.

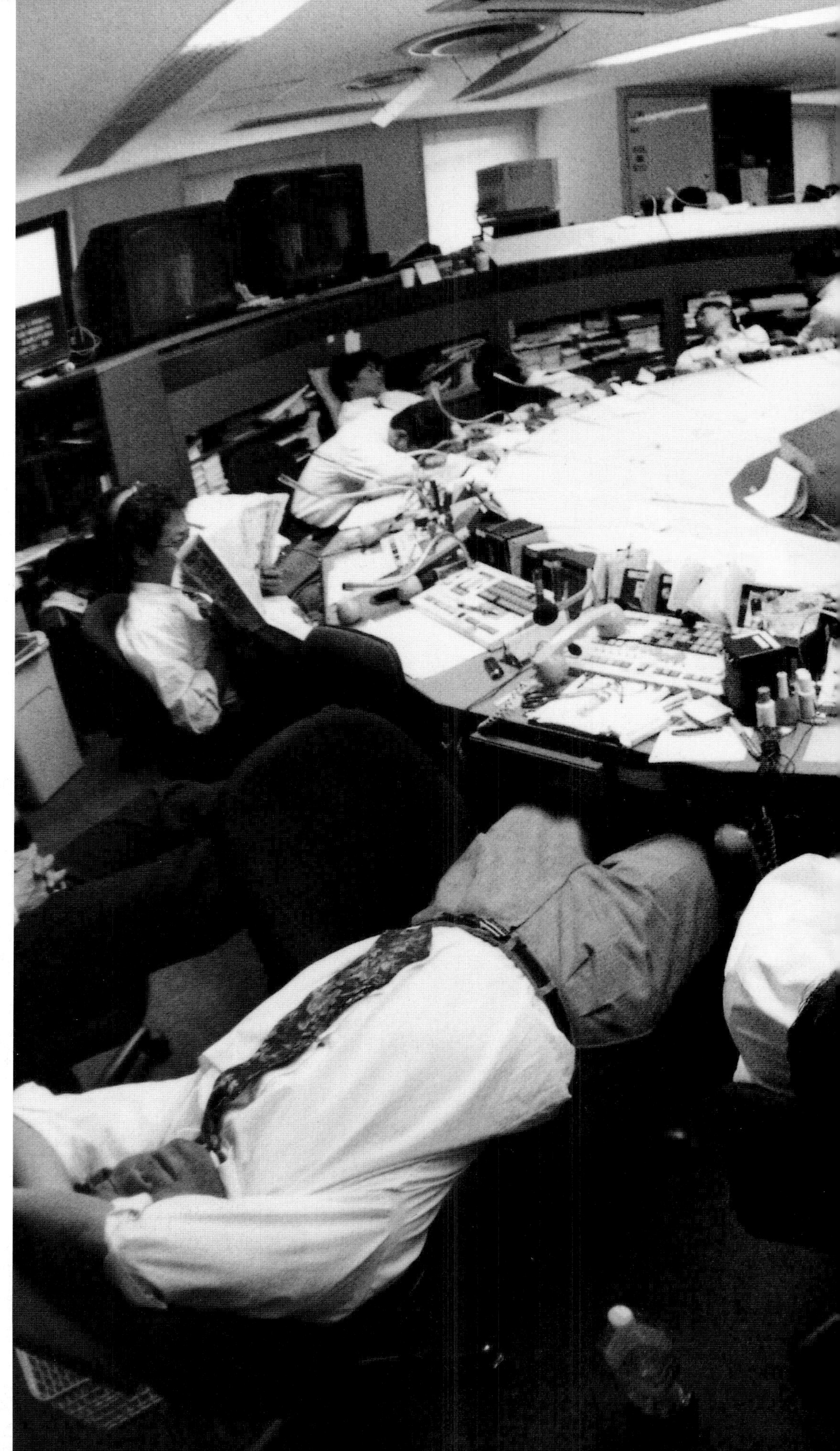

TOKYO, Japan,
7 March 1995
**Siesta at the stock
exchange**
Yen dreams.

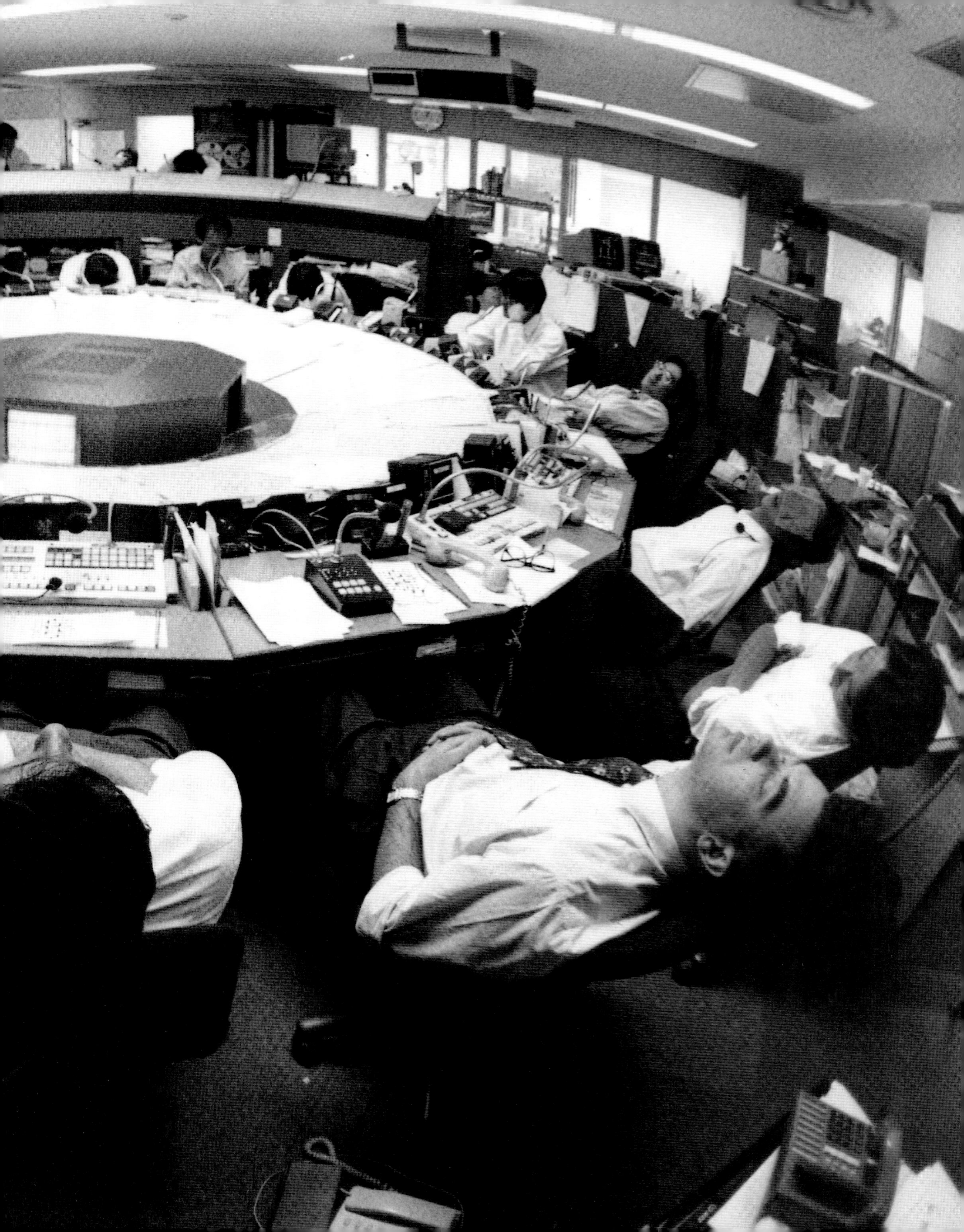

Our thanks to all the photographers who have contributed to this book:

Maria Bastone-AFP (COVER)
Joshua Roberts-AFP (p. 6, 32)
Joël Robine-AFP (p. 7)
John Redman-AFP (p. 8)
Vassili Korneyev-AFP (p. 9)
Mike Nelson-AFP (p. 10-11, BACK COVER)
Johnny Eggitt-AFP (p. 12, 13)
Patrick Rivière-AFP (p. 12)
Eric Feferberg-AFP (p. 14, 74-75)
Patrick Hertzog-AFP (p. 15, 57)
U. Waerner AFP/DPA (p. 16)
Kazuhiro Nogi-AFP (p. 17)
Gérard Julien-AFP (p. 18-19)
Vincent Amalvy-AFP (p. 20-21)
Jamal Wilson-AFP (p. 22)
Jacques Demarthon-AFP (p. 24-25, 30-31)
Jérôme Delay-AFP (p. 27)
Carlos Schiebeck-AFP (p. 28)
Vince Bucci-AFP (p. 29)
Robert Giroux-AFP (p. 33)
Jean-Loup Gautreau-AFP (p. 34)
Jean-Claude Delmas-AFP (p. 35)
Robyn Beck-AFP (p. 36-37)
Renato Rotolo-AFP (p. 38-39)
Norbert Schiller-AFP (p. 40-41)
Patrick Baz-AFP (p. 42)
Chris Wilkins-AFP (p. 43)
Stefan Ellis-AFP (p. 44)
Manuel Ceneta-AFP (p. 45)
Manoocher Deghati-AFP (p. 46)
Pascal Guyot-AFP (p. 47)
Derrick Ceyrac-AFP (p. 48, p. 78)
Ed Kosmicki-AFP (p. 49)
Georges Schneider-AFP/APA (p. 50-51)
Yoshikazu Tsuno-AFP (p. 54-55, 58, 59)
Youri Kadobnov-AFP (p. 67)
Pierre Guillaud-AFP (p. 68)
Georges Pavunic-AFP (p. 69)
Mufty Munir-AFP (p. 70-71)
Pierre Bessard-AFP (p. 76-77)
Junji Kurokawa-AFP (p. 80)
Emilio Morenatti-AFP (p. 81)
Yuri Gripas-AFP (p. 84)
Gerry Penny-AFP (p. 85)
Toru Yamanaka (p. 86-87)
STAFF-AFP (p. 52-53, 56, 62-63, 65, 66, 79)
STAFF-AFP/PA (p. 64)
AFP (p. 4, 14, 23, 26, 60-61, 72-73, 82-83)